The Scottish Football Book No 21

(Overleaf) Sandy Jardine of Rangers, was Scotland's popular choice as Player of the Year for 1974–5. A wonderful sportsman, a skilled player, Sandy Jardine is liked by everyone.
Here you see him running out – as always, with a smile – with his World Cup colleague Danny McGrain, of Celtic, for an Old Firm match.
A great season for Sandy was climaxed by his appointment as captain of Scotland in the home internationals.

THE SCOTTISH FOOTBALL BOOK NO 21

Edited by Hugh Taylor

Stanley Paul, London

Stanley Paul & Co Ltd
3 Fitzroy Square, London W1

An imprint of the Hutchinson Publishing Group

London Melbourne Sydney Auckland
Wellington Johannesburg and agencies
throughout the world

First published 1975
© Stanley Paul & Co Ltd 1975

Printed in Great Britain by litho by The Anchor
Press Ltd and bound by Wm Brendon & Son Ltd
both of Tiptree, Essex

ISBN 0 09 124490 0

CONTENTS

The Editor Says...

The Scottish Football Book comes of age this year. Yes, we're now 21. And perhaps it's fitting that this season also sees at last a brave new set-up in Scottish football. Whether the Super League will be a real hit, only time can tell. But it's well worth trying.

I feel the new three league set-up should be approached with extreme optimism for it can help to solve our problems in flagging competition and tumbling gates.

Certainly, given time, the clubs in the top ten must raise the standard of play and there won't be so many meaningless matches. It's good to see our legislators having the courage to get out of the rut and try a brave experiment.

As Rangers supremo Willie Waddell told me on the eve of the new project: 'We needed a real challenge in Scotland. We must think big. Our new set-up gives the clubs a chance to show what they can do. You can never stand still in any walk of life, let alone football. You stagnate if you don't try to progress. But now the onus is on the clubs at the top to go into action with even more flair and determination.'

Football, however, needs more than just new competitions if it is to survive in a world where more and more leisure occupations are being found.

Football needs more colour, more glamour. It must, I feel, get away from mechanical methods, from the industry of the robot, from the mathematical formula. And the words everyone in the game should heed were uttered by that great Scot, Dave Mackay, as he watched his skilful Derby County team win the English First Division last season. He declared:

'There is far too much theory in the game that is absolute rubbish.' Mackay is right and he proved that – because Derby won the title his way, playing adventurous, uninhibited football, trading goals for goals. Dave added: 'A lot of people in this game keep jobs just by organizing things to stop the opposition. When I listen to some coaches I don't know what they are talking about. I'm completely baffled. How can you coach players like Ken Dalglish, Sandy Jardine? Did Alex James and Hughie Gallacher and Gordon Smith need coaching? It's rubbish.

'The game is simple and playing method football makes a mockery of an exciting sport.'

Well, in Scotland we have never gone to the extremes of other countries but I maintain there is room for improvement, for more open football, for more bravery even here.

Clubs like Kilmarnock, although the Rugby Park men didn't make the Top Ten, showed that the fans will come hurrying back if they can watch exhilarating, attacking, entertaining soccer.

All right, I know how much victory means in football.

But surely the time has come to forget about promotion and relegation for a year or two and let the clubs concentrate on polishing their game, on playing more spectacularly, on putting the accent on attack, with real wingers and wily inside forwards and dashing centre-forwards?

I am old and grey now in this game. And I have learned one thing. It's not games you remember in football. It's not the method of Guards-drilled defences. It's players, star players, players who had verve and entertainment value, players who could use the ball, players who could shoot and dribble, strut and feint, swerve and pass accurately, keep the ball at their toes.

It's a thought the modern 'experts' should keep in mind. If we tried harder to get great players in action, players to emulate the Smiths, Jacksons, Jameses, Masons, Waddells, Tullys, Gallachers and the dozens more whose names echo still in our ears like a Gershwin song, we would be well on our way back to seeing football as the world's most fascinating sport.

Method football has killed the individual – and that's nonsense. No matter what the sport, you need stand-out experts. Why, even though, alas, wee Jimmy Johnstone of Celtic didn't make a hit last season there was always a buzz of anticipation when he came on, often as a substitute.

And can you really keep your eyes off Ken Dalglish, Sandy Jardine, Arthur Graham, Pat Stanton, Jocky Scott and a few more nowadays when you go to a game in which their clubs are playing?

I'm sure of this: nothing matters as much in football as wonderful players.

And, at the risk of repeating myself for 21 years, I must say that in Scotland we produce the best crop of all. So the game can't be all that bad.

Welcome again to another *Scottish Football Book*. I hope you enjoy it. And thank you for your letters of encouragement, advice – and criticism.

BATTLE FOR THE FLAG
Secrets of Rangers the Brave

Once again they were the Royal Rangers, the pride of the Clyde, the best team in Scotland – they were Rangers the champions.

The dream came true on Saturday March 29, 1975, at Easter Road and, on the wide, grassy slopes of that Edinburgh ground, Rangers clinched the First Division championship.

Champagne flowed in the dressing room. The legions of fans sang and danced and just wouldn't leave the stadium. Scarves and banners made glorious red, white and blue rainbows.

It was one of the greatest days in the long, illustrious Rangers history. They had won their first flag for 11 years. They were entitled to celebrate for they had been under the green shadow of their most bitter rivals Celtic for too long.

But now it was over and, even before the season had finished, Rangers had clinched the title and their days in the wilderness were ended. A 1—1 draw against Hibs was enough to make sure the flag returned to Ibrox.

Ironically, in Glasgow, Celtic that day were returning to form to beat Hearts 4—1. But it was too late. They had lost the title. Their nine-a-row record was magnificent – but there was sorrow that an epic ten-in-a-row would not happen.

It had been a fascinating title race – and the day which was probably the most important of all was January 4, 1975. A great day for Rangers. A fatal afternoon for Celtic.

Celtic's slips really began to show that day at Ibrox when they lost 3—0 to Rangers. That was the start of their decline and fall.

Before the kick-off at the Old Firm game, Celtic were in an old familiar position – at the top of the table, two points ahead of Rangers.

In losing to their old foes, however, they failed to take chances, their defence grew careless – and their confidence departed.

Later, these were the weaknesses pinpointed by manager Jock Stein as the reasons they lost the League. In contrast, Rangers became confident, played with verve and style.

The vital days were between January 4 and March 15.

On January 4, Celtic had played 20 games, won 16, drawn 2 and lost 2.

But by March 15, Celtic had played 28, won 18 drawn 4 and lost SIX.

Those six lost games spell out the capitulation of the Parkhead army. For Rangers had lost only two.

Now and again Rangers stuttered – a point dropped against Morton, another against Kilmarnock. But always Rangers hit back in determined fashion. This was the contrast:

After their draws, Rangers beat Clyde 2—1, beat Hearts 2—1, beat St Johnstone 1—0, beat Dundee 2—1.

Celtic, though, could not regain their grip and kept dropping one point after another. They lost 3—2 to Motherwell,

9

'We've done it.' No missing the joy on the face of Rangers manager Jock Wallace after his team score a goal.

drew 2—2 with Arbroath, drew 2—2 with Dumbarton, lost 1—2 to Hibs, lost 2—3 to Aberdeen, lost 0—1 to Dundee United.

Unlike Rangers, Celtic could not storm back. And it seems to me obvious that the defeat at Ibrox – their second in the League by Rangers – was responsible for the fall of the crown, for the end of a wonderful era. The sad months of January, February and March became the bleakest period in whole majestic history of the Parkhead reign at the top.

Rangers, however, weren't concerned about Celtic's worries. They had won the flag – and there is no doubt that they were good, honest, dedicated champions, perhaps not the best ever but by no means the worst in a League history which goes back to 1890–91 when Rangers and Dumbarton shared the first title.

Their resolution was admirable, for, on

It's great to be a Rangers supporter — when your team wins and you can congratulate your heroes in victory. But the fans pay a great part in Rangers' success.

the day they won the title in Edinburgh, they had lost only two matches, to Hibs and Airdrie.

And it was a joy day for their manager, the redoubtable Jock Wallace, once a jungle fighter with the KOSB in Malaya, who had led Rangers so powerfully, shaping them in his own hard image and then putting on the final polish.

But — was there something new about champion Rangers? They had been a long time in the shadows — but mainly because of the greatness of Celtic.

I felt that here were the old Rangers, stirred to the heights by the example of

Overleaf:
Another secret of the Ibrox success — hard work at training. And Sandy Jardine and Alec MacDonald are sweating it out here.

11

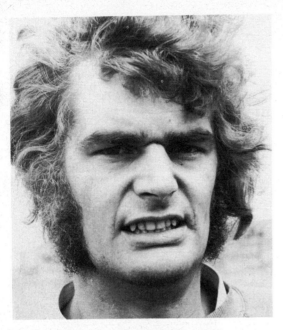

Goalkeeper of the Year? Rangers fans say so — and certainly Stewart Kennedy played a vital part in Rangers' flag march.

manager Wallace, who typifies the character of the club.

Undoubtedly there is an Ibrox mystique, a compound of strengths and weaknesses, fads and fancies, superstitions and moods. But the vital quality is club spirit. And about their play there has always been something typically Scottish — dour, if you like, an uncompromising attitude to impertinent fellows who would try to storm their stronghold, a 'wha' daur meddle wi' me' attitude.

What happened last season, I believe, is that Rangers found their good old style — a fine mixture of quiet craftsmanship as essentially Scottish as that of the shipbuilders on the nearby Clyde, neat and well ordered; of intense power; of fast, sweeping, spectacular raids.

Their style is simple but powerful — and has been so successful because of a club secret which is awe-inspiring.

Manager Wallace sums up his philosophy succinctly: 'Winning, kid, that's all Rangers want to know about.'

Yet, only a year ago, disgruntled fans were demanding Wallace's head, shouting for new leadership and even last December shareholders were hitting out at the team's performances and coaching.

What happened to change their views? Wallace switched the tactical approach. This was because he had gone to the World Cup in Germany in the summer, not so much to watch Scotland, as to study teams like Poland and Holland.

What he learned from their training and tactics rubbed off in his and the team's approach.

As Jock says: 'Power and courage have always been Ibrox assets but we played with skill, even though our enemies wouldn't admit that.'

Another factor in the Rangers League success story was — John Greig. An inspiring skipper indeed. But he had been dogged by injury.

And John was worried before the key game against Hibs — in case he couldn't play. But his nightmare ended in his shortest-ever appearance in the light blue shirt he has worn with such distinction since the day he walked into Ibrox in 1960.

In the dramatic final three minutes at Easter Road, when John — a substitute — came on to savour the success of Rangers' first success since 1964 the Ibrox captain had beaten his last enemy.

His great fear was that he would be the only Rangers skipper in a long line who had never led the club to the premier prize — a league title.

Strong man in the Rangers defence — Tom Forsyth.

Most improved Ranger — that's Colin Jackson, making a tremendous hit at centre-half.

14

Among his most treasured possession is a scrapbook where he continually looked at a picture of himself — taken with Rangers' last championship-winning team in 1964.

'If I hadn't been able to paste in a similar picture during my time as captain it would have left an empty gap, a space I dreaded,' he said. 'That didn't happen. I'm grateful to Jock Wallace for allowing me to go on near the end and share the title triumph. It was a magic moment.'

John was the sole survivor of the champions of 1964 — and not only the faces had changed since Greig's last taste of the title. Gone is the flamboyance and arrogance of the Baxter, Henderson, Brand and Wilson era.

Says Greig: 'You can't compare the sides. The last time it was a team of personalities — almost everyone an international. We aren't stars any more. It's a real team effort. Maybe that is because the game has changed. It's harder to win now. It's all about tactics.'

Greig has also lived through an unusual managerial upheaval at Ibrox. Four different bosses have named him captain since he signed on under Scot Symon. Yet Rangers needed only three other managers in the 90 years before that.

Rangers, despite the sneers that they are just a hard team, have no lack of stars — from Stewart Kennedy, a magnificent goalkeeper in the mould of Frank Swift, to the impeccable Sandy Jardine, a back of world class, from John Greig, the driving force, to Tommy McLean, so accurate with his crosses, so crisp a scorer, so artistic on the run, from the solid Colin Jackson to the devastating

Terror of defences — Derek Parlane, powerful Rangers' striker.

duo of Derek Parlane and Derek Johnstone.

Add the industrious Alec McDonald, the powerful Tom Forsyth, the clever McKean from St Mirren and the up-and-coming youngsters McDougall, O'Hara and Boyd and you can see why Rangers just laugh at foes who say they have no class.

Now Rangers have brought back Colin Stein — and it was the former Coventry City striker who scored the decisive goal against Hibs, his first club, at Easter Road.

It had been a glorious triumph for Rangers — and it had been an exciting League race.

Skipper John Greig, hit by injury, joined the Rangers backroom staff of physiotherapist Tom Craig and manager Jock Wallace to cheer on Rangers in a vital game.

They deserve the honour.

But one could not forget Celtic, at last out of the brightest of the limelight, a status to which they had been so long accustomed.

They had slipped — but they were anything but down and out and the new Premier League promises to be thrilling.

They deserve praise for what they did for Scottish football and, indeed, without the Lisbon Lions, the last decade would have been a desert.

Thanks for the memory of a tremendous team — the Celtic team of 1967 to 1970 which ranks with the best the world has ever seen.

Now Rangers go all out to prove that they, too, can supply a side to join the football pantheon of Real Madrid, Spurs of 1961, Manchester United of 1956, the great Hungarians, Brazil, Celtic and Holland.

With a man like Wallace at the helm, this goal is not impossible.

WHERE'S THE NEW JIM BAXTER FOR WORLD CUP 1978?

One of the main lessons from the World Cup in West Germany must appeal to Scottish football fans – for the lesson is that to gain top success in the 1978 series countries must find an inspirational player such as Johan Cruyff, Franz Beckenbauer or Jim Baxter.

That's the conclusion of the Technical Committee of FIFA, under the chairmanship of Walter Winterbottom, former England manager, in its analysis of the 1974 finals.

The committee, which includes Stefan Kovacs, the Rumanian who built up the original brilliant Ajax team, strongly emphasizes the importance of such players – as with Pele for Brazil – in any team which aims to lift the trophy.

With that Scots will agree. For more than any other nation we relish the artistry of the individual – because we have in our time probably had more than the rest. Think of Baxter. Who was more entrancing than Slim Jim at his peak? Not Beckenbauer, not Cruyff, not Bobby Charlton, not George Best.

Jim, however, was merely one of a long catalogue of charmers, of players who were suave, imaginative, cool – and inspired their mates to the heights.

Think of Alex James, George Hamilton Willie Mills, Tommy Walker, Bobby Walker, Torry Gillick, Tommy McInally, Willie Buchan, Tommy Gemmell (of St Mirren), Jimmy McMullan, John White, George Stevenson, Peter McKennan,

Matt Busby, Bobby Johnstone. The list is endless.

We knew how well they could play. We knew how they made a team tick, those calm cavaliers. We didn't need a new FIFA committee to tell us.

Still, it's interesting to read the report which adds something else keen Scots will appreciate – that success will be achieved only by positive attacking soccer of the kind played by the outstanding sides.

Sides like West Germany, Holland and Poland.

That we in Scotland know, too. For we have always cheered the great attacking teams, the Wembley Wizards, the Famous Five of Hibernian, the elegant Hearts of the Walker eras, the fierce, marauding Rangers of the thirties, the suave Celts of Empire Exhibition fame.

The FIFA report appears to indicate that we old-fashioned thinkers in Scotland were right all the time – right to condemn the modern robot-style, right to abhor negative, defensive play, right to maintain that the old-time attack was supreme in soccer.

The report stresses the decline in effectiveness of defensive tactics since 1966; and figures in it startlingly illustrate how Holland and West Germany in the 1974 finals mounted anything up to five times the number of penetrating attacks compared with their opponents in every match they played.

And, in conjunction with this, the experts maintain that the most effective form of attack still involves the use of outstanding flank players (see article in this book entitled Wingers — the Delight of My Life) down the touchlines, whether it is the genuine winger such as Lato (Poland) or Rep (Holland) or Grabowski (West Germany) or an overlapping full-back such as Breitner (West Germany).

The report declares that there was overwhelming evidence that flank attacks still provide the most opportunities to score.

But it also criticized the English style of play where 20 players tend to be condensed into an 'envelope' narrow strip of the field disputing possession of the ball and that too little attention is given to what to do with the ball once it has been gained.

The committee regard the use of the old-fashioned big and strong English centre-forward as outdated and point to the modern tactic of leaving the central area in front of goal free for players moving into it.

I make no apology for repeating my belief that until we return to old-fashioned ideas in style if not in sheer strength we shall be world failures.

I agree with Tom Finney, a great admirer of Scottish football, and almost Scottish in style, a waltzing toreador who left opponents — and, alas for us, often Scotland's backs — flatfooted when he says that football became a bore nine years ago when England won the World Cup and wingers and elegant inside-forwards of inspiration and culture became curios alongside the dodo and the dinosaur.

But again the top football nations are playing Finney's tune, and Smith's tune and Waddell's tune and Jackson's and Morton's tune.

Holland and Germany are attacking teams who play the old-fashioned way.

I wonder why we ever stopped that style ourselves, though it is true that in Scotland there is less emphasis than in England on method play.

Not so long ago George Best, now sadly out of football, was moaning that the game had become a bore, that there were no new stars.

What about Scotland? Where's the new Jim Baxter, the new Alex James to inspire us?

I'll tell Best — and tell the world. In Scotland we still have youngsters who relish the feel of the ball, who want to caress it, to fiddle with it, to do tricks with it, to fool opponents in a polished way, to rely on craft and guile and not power, who want to be Cruyffs and Beckenbauers — and Baxters.

Few countries have better players than Celtic's Ken Dalglish or Rangers' Sandy Jardine. And it's good to know nearly every club has at least one player with the ability to grow into a top star.

Kilmarnock have Gordon Smith, Dave Provan, Stuart McLean, Motherwell have Willie Pettigrew, Aberdeen have several great prospects including Joe Smith and Willie Miller, Dumbarton have Tom McAdam and John Bourke — and there are dozens more.

Dozens like . . .

Walker McCall, Aberdeen

Roddy McDonald, Celtic

Billy Steel, Rangers. Now with
 Dundee United

Joe Filippi, Ayr United

Ian McDougall, Rangers
Tony Higgins, Hibernian
George Anderson, Morton

A TALE OF TWO INTERNATIONAL SHOWS... Scotland's real football weakness

Two internationals inside the space of a few weeks in season 1974–5 pinpointed Scottish international football's real weakness – lack of consistency.

As always, to the Scots, with their unquenchable thirst for soccer's most romantic excitements, the game must always be a treacherous gusher, leaving them awash in champagne one moment, then drenching them in gall the next. Alas, the only certainty for us is that if the good times come, the bad are never far behind.

It has always been so. We criticize dismal performances by our international side and contrast them with the golden boys of the past, conveniently forgetting that in the twenties and thirties Scotland teams were also sensationally beaten. For instance, in 1931 we lost 5—0 to Austria in Vienna and 3—0 to Italy in Rome.

In November 1974, however, hopes had never been higher that a tartan triumph was at hand. All the land expected to see in the European Championship match against Spain a continuation of the spirited aggression that had made our unlucky exit from the 1974 World Cup a bearable pain and in October had reduced an East German team, conquerors of the World Cup winners West Germany not so long before, to tatters.

On 30 October Scotland beat East Germany 3—0 at Hampden, thus seem-ing to prove that our play in the World Cup had been no fluke, that manager Willie Ormond at last had a team which could be consistent.

A crowd of 39445 cheered themselves hoarse as the Scots humiliated the East Germans. The score could have been doubled, so superior were Scotland.

It was roses all the way. Scotland never let the Germans off the hook, hammering into attack from start to finish.

The Germans didn't like it and referee Jack Taylor, the Englishman who controlled the World Cup Final, was booed for what the fans felt was lack of action against ruthless intimidation attempts.

Indeed, Scotland's Joe Jordan was cautioned, to the disgust of the crowd – yet it wasn't until late in the second half that Gerd Kische, who had appeared to be fighting a Third World War on his own, also had his name noted.

It was a night of Scottish courage as well as skill. Scotland lost giant centre-half Jim Holton early in the game because of injury. They saw skipper Sandy Jardine, who had taken over from an unfit Billy Bremner, miss a penalty. Yet they never gave up.

Goals came from Tommy Hutchison, from another penalty, Ken Burns, a success as deputy for Holton, and Ken Dalglish. And East Germany, verging on greatness in the World Cup, were humiliated.

24

All night toasts were drunk – and most praise went to a newcomer, young Graeme Souness, of Middlesbrough.

We all thought a star had been born, for the lad played with a subtlety the Scots love, using the ball brilliantly and delicately.

The twenty-one-year-old from Edinburgh had been in the shadows at Tottenham Hotspur and was transferred to Middlesbrough for a £30 000 fee, hardly eyebrow raising in these days when a £100 000 transfer hardly is worth a headline.

Souness attributed his success to the coaching of his midfield colleague Bobby Murdoch, the former Celtic and Scotland star, whose long passes were missed by both his old teams.

'Souness will do us a real turn,' we all said – and sipped another drink.

A tartan rainbow nudged blue Scottish skies. We were on top of the world. A few critics, including myself, were lambasted for asking mildly if success hadn't gone to our heads, if we shouldn't consider the fact that East Germany hadn't tried all that hard – except physically – and weren't a patch on the side which had done so well in the World Cup.

And so to the more important match on 20 November, with Spain, a competitive match, a match we had to win to give us the boost we needed in our efforts to qualify for the final stages of the European Championship, as the former Nations Cup was known.

Our tails were up. The thought of defeat brought laughs. Even Denis Law just retired and certainly an expert who ought to know, joined in with a prediction of a comfortable Scottish victory, saying: 'Spain will be a bit frightened of us after seeing the result we had against East Germany. They'll also be frightened of the Hampden atmosphere.'

Even though Scotland were without injured stars Holton, Davie Hay, Danny McGrain and Martin Buchan, there was no gloom. After all, wasn't Billy Bremner back, the inspiring skipper whose fire and authority had earned such praise in West Germany? And the fans couldn't wait to see how he teamed up with Souness.

Anyhow, Spain were also at half-strength and on 20 November, one of those Glasgow winter nights that are as raw as a hatchet wound, 92 000 supporters forsook the warmth of home, pub and club, ready to cheer another fine Scottish victory that would take us to global fame at last.

And what a start Scotland made. Billy Bremner scored early, and Spain were on the ropes when they gave away a penalty. That, though, was the beginning of the end for Scotland. Tommy Hutchison looked aghast when his kick was saved, Spain took heart, Scotland lost the place, and the visitors, who had come looking for a draw, won 2—1, exposing gaps in the Scottish defence.

And it was back to the lament in the glens, the greeting in the pubs, the demand for heads to fall. The old, old story of disaster following in the footsteps of triumph.

As we glowed in the warm light of victory over East Germany, so we wallowed in tears in the aching pain of defeat by Spain.

No half-measures for the Scots, who want to be in either ecstasy or anguish, who seem to find as much joy in a dirge as in a victory march.

Overleaf:
This is what the Scottish fans love to see – the victory salute. Alas, it isn't often we can cheer the boys in blue as we did here after they beat Czechoslovakia to qualify for the World Cup finals in West Germany.

25

What went wrong? The saddest aspect was that Spain were no Holland or West Germany, no more than a sensibly organized team with an economic method and enough nerve to withstand the brief exuberance of Scotland's initial assaults.

Yet how did we dare, a small country like Scotland, to believe we could scale the heights lacking so many of our stars? And Billy Bremner, who had missed so much of the season because of injury, was nothing like his true self – a player who began like a lion and became in all too short a space a breathless, toothless terrier.

Souness, too, was a sad disappointment, never in the game, too slow to make room for himself and others.

But why go on?

Our tale never changes. Up in the clouds one minute – down in the depths the next.

An expert, close look at our international set-up is needed. These two results merely illustrate a story was old as Scottish soccer itself – and the reactions of officials, writers and fans maintain our football's tradition of summits and troughs, of dismal spasms of mediocrity and the flash of outstanding players and teams who lunge gleefully at the throats of any opponents, West Germany, England or Luxembourg, who happen to be in the way.

No consistency in this pattern.

Alas for every Baxter, every James, every Morton, there are scores of plain players.

Scottish fans love to see goals – like this one scored by Birmingham's Kenny Burns against East Germany.

But this is what we too often see – international defeats and misses. Here Joe Jordan is baulked by Spanish goalkeeper Iribar and Spain went on to win.

And perhaps the basic fault in Scottish football is that we do not have early control. This is the pet theory of Willie Fernie, the Kilmarnock manager who was once one of the most mesmerizing players of all time, a Celtic wizard whose dribbling was a thing of joy, whose control was breathtaking.

Fernie has this to say about Scottish football: 'We have been overtaken by the rest of the world and have lived in a land of illusion. Nearly all South American and Continental players have the gift of early control – that is, they can trap the ball with chest, leg, foot much more deftly that we can.

'Perhaps our climate is against us. Our players on muddy surfaces can wait until the ball lands, plump in the muck, and it's easy to stop it with their feet. It doesn't bounce about. But Continentals on hard surfaces must always try to beat the bounce, get to the ball and kill it before it lands.'

Willie could be right, for our great players seemed to live in an age when soccer was learned on the tricky surface of a street or piece of waste ground.

And don't forget that changes in styles of football aren't mainly a matter of tactics or temperament. Equipment has also played its part.

The 1950s saw, for instance, the introduction of the new synthetic football which did not soak up water. An experiment has shown that after six hours soaking the modern ball is unchanged in weight, the old-style leather ball half as heavy again.

Now there is no problem about kicking or heading the ball in even the worst weather.

This change has helped to even out international competition from the time when British teams were sure to win if it was muddy, likely to lose if the ground was hard, the ball light.

And it's another miss. This time centre-half McQueen fails to pierce the Spanish defence.

Ormond has to persevere with the style which earned Scotland so much praise in Germany. He tried to combine the new with the old, to evolve a pattern.

Chopping and changing won't help. He must try to bring on a side organically pruning cannily, hoping for the bloom to bring real colour to our international football.

But we must face facts. A win over England, a draw with Brazil — so what? These results don't make us world champions, but neither should a defeat from Spain make us feel soccer outcasts.

We are a small country in a huge world of football. We have no divine right to victory. We have given much to the game.

We must now be happy with a moderate result — and certainly no country makes more drama out of football than Scotland.

Let's face it. We enjoy the anguish just as much as the ecstasy. . . .

CALL IN THE INVISIBLE MAN!
and make football brighter...

Excitement was the name of the game in Scotland in season 1974–5. Our teams didn't make a hit in Europe, or even in the Texaco Cup against English opponents, and inconsistency marred our international performances – but in the fight for places in the Top Ten super league there was action galore, open football and an upsurge in entertainment.

No one was keener in the quest to bring back the missing fans to the terracings than the players and here are some of their views about how football can be improved:

John Greig of Rangers: 'The secret of any good team is to incorporate players with individual flair into the team pattern. No manager should stamp out individuality. Anyone who stereotypes a team should remember that's it's individuals like Pele, Cruyff and Muller who draw the crowds.

'And the fans today are far more sophisticated than they were ten years ago. They can't be kidded. It's good to hear them discuss the latest tactics.

'The biggest annoyance is defensive football and I suppose the coaches must take responsibility for that.

'I realize some clubs must play to their own resources, but surely it is worth having a go and being beaten than defending and driving the fans away.'

Joe Harper of Hibs: 'The game is crying out for wingers, men prepared to take on defenders, get past them and hoist the ball over into the goal area.

'The penalty box is where excitement begins and ends in this game. If you have plenty of action around the goalkeeper the game is bound to be exciting for the fans and the players.

'Football also needs characters and too much emphasis is still placed on defence, especially by clubs playing away from home.

'I'm not in favour of changing the rules. I keep hearing and reading about how exciting the game was back in the fifties when Hibs had their Famous Five and Hearts had Conn, Bauld and Wardhaugh. Well, these lads played to the same rules as we do and if they could make the game attractive for the fans there's no reason why we shouldn't be able to . . . if only we get back to playing real wingers again.'

Dom Sullivan of Clyde: 'There's no room in football for the robot style. The fans don't want to see machines carrying out exercises. They want to see excitement and that means letting players take chances on the park.

'It's all very well managers saying that they can't afford to take chances and lose games, but the onus is on them to let players show flair.'

Jim Cruickshank of Hearts: 'The game has lost out because it has become too technical. The accent now is more on stopping goals than knocking them in

31

and that's all wrong. The current trend has drifted away from wingers, inside-forwards, centre-halfs and full backs.

'Now everybody is an all-purpose player The modern style stifles characters. Perhaps we should return to the old 2—3—5 set-up.'

Billy McNeill of Celtic: 'Football is a team game and I think it's silly to talk about the sport being more attractive with 'characters'. Players need room within a system to show flair but it is sometimes very difficult playing with a character.

'I think, however, the standard in Scotland has gone up.

'It might be a thought on the subject of attendances to try to play more matches at night, perhaps on Fridays.

'As a player, I feel it's a better setting, with more excitement, playing in a night game.'

Willie Young, Aberdeen: 'The first improvement is in the hands of the managers and coaches. The fans want to see attacking football. The game should be allowed to flow more and the advantage rule could be better used by some referees. I am certain you would get better soccer if there were points for goals.

'Perhaps an extra point for a team scoring three or more would also be a good idea. Then if a game was 4—3 the losing side would take something out of it for the entertainment they had given.'

Of all those views, the most important, I feel, is that of Willie Young, the Aberdeen centre-half.

How can football be improved? The stars give their views:

John Greig, of Rangers: 'Everyone must have a go.'

32

'The game should be allowed to flow more and the first improvement is in the hands of the managers and the coaches,' he says. He's right.

It's no use crying for the return of wingers, the old system, the wizard-of-dribble character who used to delight us.

Football has progressed. And many teams today play more entertaining football than even that of the Wembley Wizards, believed by all Scots to be the golden boys of our greatest soccer era.

No Scottish team can compare with Bayern Munich, Barcelona or Juventus.

And these teams have combined the brilliant skills of world-class stars with a new conception of tactics — a conception which still seems to bewilder the British, even though, I admit, we are making progress in modern methods.

Yet the new look on tactics was vividly explained back in 1955 — almost twenty years before the description 'total football' became the key words of the 1974 World Cup in West Germany — by Austrian-born Willi Meisl, brother of Hugo, the supremo of Austrian football.

Meisl in his famous book *Soccer Revolution* described the style of the future, 'The Whirl' — and that is how the best foreign teams play today.

Meisl called the Whirl a form of tactics to end all soccer systems by setting individuality free once again and

Billy McNeill, of Celtic, seen with Liverpool's Bill Shankly at his benefit match: 'Why don't we play on Fridays?'

said it consisted of a team pattern based on all-round ability.

To execute the Whirl, he wrote, every player must be able to tackle anybody else's job temporarily without any ado. The Whirl, then, is a non-stop switch comprising all ten field players — a series of switches on a fast-running belt, running in all directions simultaneously, as it were.

To perform it, you must have players of the highest class — and you must be adept at what the Hungarians, the masters of the plan, called the Invisible Man approach.

In short, to be a top team you must have players who have found the secret of running off the ball. I maintain, like Meisl, that if there is a simple gauge for the top footballer — apart from perfect technique which must be considered a presupposition — it is his play without the ball. How does he 'live' with the game, follow it when a partner or an opponent is in possession of the ball? How does he place himself instinctively? Watch this and you will soon know who is great, who is average, who is mediocre — and who is near hopeless.

Clubs like Barcelona have reached the peak of success because they have so many great players who are so good off the ball, seem to lurk in the shadows and then suddenly hit hard.

They have also learned something we in Scotland don't always appreciate: That to speed up the game it must not be forgotten that the ball can be faster than the fastest sprinter, that it is blessed also with more stamina than the toughest Marathon runner. The principle is: Let the ball do the running.

Willie Young, of Aberdeen: 'The game should be allowed to flow more.'

The great clubs have condemned the idea of playing to a prefabricated formula which forces the game into a rut. Of course, they also make their plans, but they drill in only a few basic moves and leave it to the aptitude or, in the cases of Cruyff and Beckanbauer, the genius of the individual to vary them according to necessity or possibilities.

And the great clubs make better use than anyone else of the Invisible Man.

The Invisible Man? It's the 'missing link' in football, the element of telepathy which puts the final stamp on the world-class teams — and a theory on which our coaches should be working to make soccer really attractive.

Briefly, it's all concerned with running off the ball, of finding the way to link their players together mentally so that they seem to be telepathic.

No one used the Invisible Man arproach better than the Hungarians of 1953. Time and time again Kocsis and Puskas broke through the centre with the English centre-half Johnston nowhere to be seen. It was a combination of the Whirl, changing places with the man to whom the player passed the ball, and the Invisible Man.

It's running off the ball. When the Hungarian right-half gave the ball to his outside-right he ran to the right wing. Then number 7 gave to number 4 (now on the wing) and ran back to the touchline. Then he crossed and ran to the centre. Where was the opposing left back? He might have followed number 7 to centre-forward, number 9, in which case there was no effective left back. Or he might have remained in position and was marking number 4. But — who was then marking number 7, the new centre-forward.

The Invisible Man is the man with the ball, who passes to whoever he wishes — but must run to take that man's place, even while that man is making a similar pass to another player.

It springs from the wall pass — at which the old Hibernian team were so adept. Call it the playground wall move, if you like — hitting the ball to a stationary colleague and getting it back.

The Invisible Man technique takes this much further. With the wall pass you link two men together — but this is easily spotted as the two players complete their move in full view of the defender.

So — bring in the Invisible Man and make a basic one–two–three, with the third man coming from behind and running into a position on the blind side of the defender.

The top teams develop more and more of those basic combinations, linking groups of three and then four players together.

In Scotland we take combination play a little further than the wall pass.

Bring in the Invisible Man and we will have more sophisticated and entertaining football.

WINGERS-THE DELIGHT OF MY HEART Even though they receive a left-handed compliment from a famous coach

Right-wingers have always been my favourite players. I loved the waspish swiftness of Jimmy Delaney, the elegant flair of Alec Jackson, the audacious attacks of Willie Waddell, the poetry of Gordon Smith. Even in this modern age, when wingers don't seem to fit into a method style, there is nothing in football to match the excitement of watching an on-form Jimmy Johnstone perform his magic on the right touchline.

Scotland has always been rich in wing positions, especially on the right, and in our folklore the names of that famous breed of outside-rights, headed by the remarkable Bobby Templeton, said to be the most fascinating of them all, compare with any of today's greats.

Yes, how I loved them – the artists, the raiders, the magicians of the right touchline.

To me they were incomparable, the most gifted of all players.

So it was rather a shock, when I was covering the 1974 World Cup in West Germany, to listen to one of football's most able and respected coaches, George Raynor, the Englishman who had done so much for Sweden as their manager.

George laid it squarely on the line that while he agreed that right-wingers were football's most brilliant personalities, that was due mainly to the fact that left backs were usually the weakest men in most teams.

I was rather hurt. Because the conversation had started well enough for me and my theory that right-wingers are the men who matter most.

George had said that while Cruyff and Beckenbauer might be the best players in the World Cup, they were hardly the players most likely to win the tournament. 'You should,' remarked George, 'put your money on a right-winger to score the winning goal in the final.'

I purred and George praised the World Cup's magnificent right-wingers: Uli Hoeness of West Germany, Johnny Rep of Holland and Georgio Lato of Poland.

Raynor is a man who knows what he's talking about. He knew more about World Cup football than anyone else in Germany in the summer of 1974, for he was boss of Sweden in 1950 when they were third in the tournament and in 1958 when they lost in the final to Brazil.

'It's my belief that right-wingers are the men most likely to be dangerous,' he went on. 'Look at the World Cup history and you'll see my theory is right.' And here's the record:

In 1950 outside-right Chiggia of Uruguay scored the goal that mattered.

In 1954 outside-right Rahn of West

Germany got two goals in the final against Hungary.

In 1958 Garrincha of Brazil was the great man in the World Cup Final.

In 1970 Jairzinho of Brazil was the right-winger and the most menacing player on the field.

Of 1966, however, George shook his head sadly.

'That was Alf Ramsey's year,' he said, 'and he didn't like wingers, did he?'

But 1974 saw the World Cup turning again into a wonderful world for wingers. The biggest boost for the touchline artists was the return of West Germany's Hoeness, a blond terror who tears down the touchline like a new Willie Waddell.

And everyone was in ecstasy over the performances of Argentina's tiny tot, Rene Houseman, who showed that the smaller they are, the better they seem to be.

Just as I was considering that Scotland would have done better in the World Cup if they had played Jimmy Johnstone on the right touchline, Raynor that wise old Englishman, sobered my glowing recollections of wing wizards with this intriguing view:

'Of course,' he said with a twinkle in his eye, 'the real reason that right wingers are the most menacing players isn't necessarily because they are the best players.

'No, it could be that left-backs are usually the weakest men in most teams.

'That's because there are not all that many of them and left-footed players

Celtic's Paul Wilson — a left-winger who has all the arts and crafts of the old-time greats.

Iain MacDonald, of Dundee United, is a touchline terror; with skill and pace, and is making a fine comeback after a depressing spell with Rangers.

tend to be elegant but lacking real drive, fire and strength.

'It's the same in cricket. Left-handers have grace and style but it's the right-handers who score the runs. Left-handed bowlers may look good but it's usually the right-handed bowlers, especially fast bowlers, who get the wickets.

'So in football. Good left-backs are hard to come by.'

I respect George Raynor. But I'm not all that sure his theory is correct. After all, I've seen many fine left-backs in my day, as well as splendid right-wingers — Sammy Cox of Rangers, Harry Haddock of Clyde, Joe Nibloe of Kilmarnock, Tommy Gemmell of Celtic, to mention only a few.

And who could tackle more strongly than Sammy Cox, as superb at half-back as he was in defence, and who could kick the ball harder and longer than Nibloe?

Anyhow, I won't change my mind that right-wingers were the most entertaining of all footballers — and will be again, I'm sure. For the World Cup in Germany showed that wingers can still play a part, even if they didn't score the winning goal in the final, and if our home coaches take a hint, forget the brainwashing of the Ramsey era, and try to make the game more open and attractive, they will once again put the accent on feeding the wing terrors with the type of passes they love.

It's perhaps true that nostalgia and statistics have always exercised a greater fascination for cricket lovers than for football followers, but I believe the experts of today should pay more attention to how the game was played in the past — and the recent past, at that.

Even in the fifties football still showed the exuberance of youth without constraints and caution of today's stern manhood.

What went wrong with soccer? Has it advanced too much? Certainly football, socially, technically and tactically, in planning and training and in the stream-lining of playing kit and equipment has advanced with great strides in the last decade.

Progress? Again, perhaps. For what has gone out of the game is – fun. As that famous manager Joe Mercer said: 'Compared to the humour of our days, when I see the boys running out of the tunnel now they all look as if they are on the way to Vietnam.'

And I maintain that most of the fun went out of the game not because of the strains and tension of the times being reflected in all walks of British life but because of tactics which shy at the thought of one winger, never mind two.

Flourish and thrills were added to football by the pairings of great wingers, Smith and Ormond, Matthews and Finney and, abroad, Czibor and Budai for Hungary, Garrincha and Zagalo for Brazil, Hamrin and Skoglund for Sweden, Rahn and Schaefer for Germany.

No wonder there was so much colour in the fifties – for wingers were the supreme creators of goals.

I maintain that the disappearance of wingers left football looking more anaemic to the spectator. Even in Scotland, where wingers lingered, there was an accent on method play and so the game was robbed of those goals that are the red corpuscles of the game.

I hope we are on the way back. I hope more and more wingers, always the pride and joy of Scotland, come to the fore.

Let me end with this vivid description of what a real winger really is:

One of the crispest and speediest wingers in football is Arthur Duncan of Hibs, seen here in a joust with Peter McCloy of Rangers.

'You may have your own plan on how to stop him – but so has your manager, coach and all your team-mates. "Make him do this," says one. "Make him do that," says another. "Stay close to him . . . Keep away from him . . . Watch him . . . Ignore him" . . . It goes on. . . .

'Finally you get there and the phantom with the number seven on his back gets the ball. Unlike most other players, he does not try to avoid you, comes wriggling his casual way towards you. You tense and watch that ball. Now he's within your reach and he sways outward to his right, like a snake. He's going down the wing, you think, and lunge forward with your left foot to block the ball. All of a sudden – whsst! – this blur goes past you on the inside and your eyes pop up in amazement.

'He's got the ball again – but this time you are ready for him. He's not going to get away with that again. So, as he sways leisurely outwards to his right again, you tackle forward, this time with your right foot to stop him coming inside and – whsst! – the blur goes past on the outside.

'Then – whsst! – there he goes again and you are lying on the ground and saying to yourself: "To hell with it. I've had enough of this fellow." '

That was Danny Blanchflower writing about the great Stanley Matthews. That's a real winger for you. Don't you wish like me we had a new Stan or a new Gordon Smith or Willie Waddell or Alan Morton?

Who can forget wee Willie Henderson, that great Rangers right-winger, endowed with all the qualities which endeared wingers to the hearts of the Scottish fans.

Overleaf:

The unforgettable Jimmy Johnstone of Celtic – seen in the match against East Germany.

43

HOT PROPERTIES: An attacker and a defender are the finds of the season

Despite failures on the international front, despite complaints that football is faltering, there is a bright feature to the season — the fact that Scotland still produces brilliant players.

When you look back down memory lane you realise what a magnificent contribution Scotland has made to football. No country has given more masters to soccer. No country has had such a wealth of really great players — in all positions.

And, thank Heaven, we still do, still breed lads who can achieve world fame.

There were several outstanding hits on the 1974–5 parade — and I've chosen two who seem to me destined to go right to the top.

The hottest properties of the season are a striker and a defender: Willie Pettigrew of Motherwell, and Gordon McQueen, of Leeds United.

McQueen has arrived. Pettigrew is on the way up. I think they were the finds of the season.

The changing moods of football are best reflected by the difference in styles of the centre-forward or, if you prefer the new jargon, striker.

In the old days, when the game was much more physical — which will give food for thought for those of the younger generation who consider that the Storeys, the Forsyths, the Barry's and the Murrays can really make their presences felt — and forwards had a good chance of being kicked over the stand, never mind being only ruthlessly tackled, centre-forwards were burly individualists who had to batter their way to supremacy. They had to charge with heavy shoulders, bundle opponents out of the way and shot with awesome ferocity even if accuracy was sadly lacking.

Then came the new age of science. With the game growing more elegant, centre-forwards had to change their tactics. We had the Gallachers, the Reillys, the Baulds, the Thorntons — remarkable assets to the art of centre-forward play, for they were jack-o'-lanterns who confused their opponents by unexpected entries.

The battering-ram approach was out. Leaders weren't really leaders at all. They were high intellectuals, participating in an enchanting pattern play, unselfish, more often content to make rather than to take goals.

But the policy of leading from behind died because all too often teams gave the appearance of having two inside-lefts

Here he is, Scotland's dynamic new striker, Willie Pettigrew, of Motherwell.

and one inside-right (or vice-versa) but no centre-forward.

With the advent of robot play, teams tried to get goals via a double striking partnership, based on the old style – two big fellows bashing in to try to beat the strongest and best disciplined defences football had known.

Then came the West Germans, perhaps the best international team of all, certainly the most effective if not always the most spectacular or entertaining.

With them came Gerd Muller – and a new style of leader. Seldom seen in a match. Seldom applauded for trickery or scintillating dribbling. But always the most menacing attacker in football.

Because Muller is lethal. Because he hits at the right time. Because he pops up out of nowhere. Because he can score not only with vicious shots but with half-hit jabs. Because he is the ideal foil for more spectacular colleagues.

Muller is the type of leader every club, every country seeks.

And that's why Willie Pettigrew, of Motherwell, will soon be the hottest property in Scottish football.

Willie is the new scoring sensation – and he's only 21.

He can be the new Muller. He talks like the famous German . . .

'I know my limitations. I've no false ideas about being a ball player. I'm not the sort who can hold on to the ball. When I get inside the 18-yard line I never put a team-mate in possession. That would be passing the buck. I'm the boy who's supposed to be good at scoring so I have a go. Every time.'

Like Muller, he is indebted to skilled aid from cultured mates – mates like the artistic, shrewd Bobby Graham.

'Bobby is a wonderful partner,' says Willie. 'He knows all the moves and has magnificent control and passing ability. He certainly lays them on for me and

we hit it off from the start in our partnership.'

Like so many other fine players, Willie has known heartbreak in football.

He trained with Motherwell as a schoolboy – but no one seemed to want him and he drifted away. Then he was a provisional signing with Hibs – but he was never called up.

Pettigrew moved to East Kilbride Juniors and his scoring touch came shining through. He scored 43 goals – and Motherwell came along to ask him to sign.

They didn't have to ask him twice. 'I jumped at the chance,' Willie said. No wonder. For he is a home-town boy. He is never far away from Fir Park. From his house, he can see the floodlights and

Gordon McQueen, new superstar of Leeds United.

48

his part-time job in the offices of Motherwell secretary Jack McGraw is even nearer the ground.

'Being a Motherwell boy born and bred,' he says, 'I realise just how important it is to the town to have a successful team. Being surrounded by fans of my team keeps me on my toes. If I have a bad game, there's no way I don't get to know about it.'

Delighted with Willie's success is manager Willie McLean: 'If I had to be pinned down to a single factor for our good run last season it would be Willie's ability to keep putting the ball in the net.

'Before this, the team were playing just as well — but weren't taking their chances. Pettigrew solved this problem.'

Most clubs in Britain would love a

Pettigrew — a lad who can put the ball into the net.

Argument still rages among Rangers supporters as to whether George Young, Willie Woodburn or Davie Meiklejohn was the supreme centre-half. Meiklejohn was a superb, versatile player, say some. Woodburn was more incisive in the tackle, maintain others. Ah, but Young was the more commanding, declare his supporters.

All I know about this controversy is that Meiklejohn, Young and Woodburn, the giants of Rangers in the great club's most spectacular eras, were the best centre-halves I ever saw — perhaps the best centre-halves the world has seen, superior to anyone, at home and abroad, when outstanding players, English, Irish and foreign, filled this position.

Gordon McQueen in action for Scotland against Spain at Hampden.

Rangers have always been noted for centre-halves – but I wonder if they regret that they missed a youngster who may develop into the greatest centre-half of all time?

The name? Gordon McQueen. And right away there will be the usual moans from the anti-Anglos that as soon as a Scot goes south he becomes a world-beater while, in fact, there are far better players at home.

McQueen, however, has become a favourite with the Hampden fans – and when you realize England's professional players have named him as the best centre-half in England after only three years down south and two seasons in the Leeds United first team you must concede that this tall, leggy young man is unique.

There can scarcely ever have been such a swift rise to fame. Gordon left St Mirren for Leeds as a raw, inexperienced, thin lad, with many alleged experts wondering just why the heck United had chosen him to be Jackie Charlton's successor.

Certainly Rangers never thought for a moment that they had missed a star and probably didn't even remember that Gordon had once trained at Ibrox. For a week. And got only a 20-minute spell in a testimonial match Rangers played in Fife. Rangers shook their heads and Gordon headed back to the Junior club Largs Thistle.

Then his luck changed. Alex Wright was manager of St Mirren and signed McQueen from Largs after Liverpool as well as Rangers had turned him down. 'He was rough and ready,' said Alex, 'but I realized he had talent. Even when he lasted only two minutes in his first appearance for St Mirren.

'He played in a friendly against Crystal Palace, who had just signed Alan Birchenall for £100 000. But we had to take him off because he was so nervous that he became sick.'

But Gordon's skill told in the end. He became a splendid St Mirren player. English clubs began to take an interest. But Leeds manager Don Revie got Gordon – at the bargain price of £40 000.

Now he's one of the country's richest as well as best footballers. With St Mirren, he earned £25 a week. Now when Leeds are playing big mid-week games Gordon can pay £200 a week – in Income Tax.

Now he's a superstar but still a modest lad and he likes to pay tribute to his mentors, Syd Owen and Jackie Charlton, both former England centre-halves. 'Jackie talked me through reserve game after reserve game. Syd had me back at the ground all day and every day,' he says. 'They taught me so much and I'm grateful.'

At 22, Gordon McQueen has the world at his feet. Voted the top man in England, he has played for his country and will be fighting fiercely to make the Scottish centre-half position his own.

LAW'S ORDER FOR SOCCER...
Go back to the scintillating sixties

Away back in 1958, that distinguished Irish internationalist Danny Blanchflower said to me ruefully: 'If that's him at eighteen, I wouldn't like to play against him when he's twenty-four.'

'Him' was Denis Law, then a slim, blond, whiffy-haired youth and, at eighteen, the youngest player to be capped for Scotland since R. S. McColl sixty years before.

There was no heroic, attacking role for Denis in that game. Although later he was often accused of being an individualist, happier playing in his own wonderful style than sticking to a team pattern, he had, on that occasion, played strictly to the pre-match order he had received – worrying and harrying the great Blanchflower off his game and thus disrupting the Irish attacking rhythm.

Many people didn't like the roughness Law, a stripling, displayed on that occasion. But Law did what he was told – and did it so well that Blanchflower played little part in that Scotland–Ireland international.

It was, however, hardly a romantic start to Law's international career – for in the previous game, his first for Scotland, against Wales at Cardiff he had been reprimanded by the referee for showing signs of retaliation.

And veterans sniffed and felt that Law rather too much resembled two turbulent characters – in appearance, Tommy Steele, the raucous entertainer of the day, and, in play, the furious Billy Steel.

But Denis explained it all like this: 'Well, frankly, I had to show that I had guts and skill. After all, when I was sent from Aberdeen to Huddersfield I was frail and slight and wore thick specs.

'Maybe I was too brash, but I was on my way up and I was going to let everyone know I was around, even Danny Blanchflower, who, really, was a hero of mine.'

But that's the Law few people remembered when the great Denis retired in season 1974–5 after one of the most colourful soccer careers in history.

It was a sad day for the Scots because Law had become football's D'Artagnan, an audacious attacker in an age when heroes and heroics had gone out of fashion – had turned sharply from being a wrecker, stopping the opposition at all costs, into being a match-winner, a man who, like Rob Roy or Robin Hood, defied overwhelming odds by sheer force of physique, skill and imagination and achieved the seemingly impossible.

Law, at thirty-four, gave up playing because he wanted to get out while he was still at the top – Scotland's most-capped player, who had taken part in a World Cup and the man who has scored more English Cup goals than anyone else.

How good a player was Law? He had fans who idolized him, others who felt

he relied too much on physique. To me, he was the best in the world as an inspiration, a scorer, a saver of forlorn hopes. There was an electric touch about his play. His reflexes were superb, his swerve stupendous, his acceleration breathtaking. No striker could rise in the air like Law, a pouncing puma. He was a man's man, a footballing buccaneer out for death or glory, tremendously gifted athletically. No player in history

more earned tributes like these when he retired:

From Donald Ford of Hearts: 'He is the greatest character Scottish football has known, incredible, highly intelligent and with a fantastic sense of humour.'

From John Greig of Rangers: 'As a young player, Denis was my idol. When I later played alongside him in a Scottish side he was out of this world.'

From Bill Shankly, also retired as a manager: 'Denis is one of the greatest players of all time. He had everything and he could do anything and play anywhere. He had pace, skill, heading ability and he could score goals. He possessed the heart of a lion.'

Denis Law has retired — but the memory lingers on. And here are two glimpses of the great Law in action, pictures that show his astonishing reflexes:

No one could get higher in the air than Denis, leaping above the England defence at Hampden.

No one could score more spectacular goals than Denis. Here's one — against Ireland, also at Hampden.

Certainly he was beloved of every schoolboy — for kids wanted to play like him. They also were entranced by his career, which read like a novel. . . .

From spindly-legged lad to soccer hero . . . a superb athlete transferred from Manchester City, to which club he

had gone after service with Huddersfield Town, to the bright lights and glamour of Italian soccer with Turin . . . hailed by the vociferous Latin fans as a forward with the speed of a gazelle, the striking power of a barracuda . . . a Scottish soldier of fortune . . . drama and disillusion in Italy, where he felt his style was cramped in the defensive set-up, the failure to become the militant monk demanded of Italian stars . . . back to Britain and Manchester United, who paid a then record £116000 for Law in 1962 . . . always glamour . . . sometimes disappointment . . . back to Manchester City . . . then recall to Scotland's World Cup team in 1974.

He made foes, who didn't like his brashness. But most of all he had admirers because of his football ability there was never any doubt. And his cheek and lack of respect for the opposition went a long way in making him the player he was.

And when order came to Law he became the most feared forward in the world.

Law insists he is finished with football. 'Obviously,' he told me, soon after he brought down the curtain on a glorious career spanning almost twenty years, 'I thought about keeping in the game as manager, trainer, or coach but I don't want to move from my home in Manchester. It was great playing for Scotland but I like living in Manchester. I am in business with a friend and I still train at a local gymnasium.'

Law, who never watched matches when he was unfit because he got too excited, now enjoys a game and can sit back, he says, and enjoy the play.

And Denis still likes Scottish soccer. The man with fifty-five caps for his country says: 'Scottish football is far more entertaining than in England. People who knock our game don't know what they are talking about.

'I've been around English football for a long time, and it is my firm belief that Scotland has its soccer priorities right – England hasn't.

'Indeed, I believe that some time soon English football is going to take a hard look at its problems and decide to move towards the Scottish system or go bust.

'Individuality is being suppressed in England and the crowds are staying away because of it. Managers hold the key. They are depriving fans of good attacking football to keep themselves in jobs.

'If I was a manager I would abandon stereotyped football and rely on entertainment. As it is, English bosses are stifling the game to such an extent that it is crucial they stop method football.'

And there will be for Law applause as loud as when he scored a spectacular goal as he continues: 'England's World Cup win in 1966 was a terrible thing in the end. At the time it was a fine result. Gates were dropping and victory for England brought fresh enthusiasm to the game. But the method in which that win was achieved has haunted the game ever since in England.

'Everyone jumped on the bandwagon and teams were not able to do their own thing. They became dull, unentertaining and eventually the fans got wise and stopped attending games.

'That is why Scottish soccer has the edge over the English. I know some bosses up here have put defensive tactics into their play, but, on the whole, Scottish play is more open and honest.'

And let's leave Law, who provided us with so much drama and spectacle and glamour, saying: 'I have a simple solution to the entertainment problem. Let's revert to pre-1966 days.

'Our Manchester United team of the sixties never worried about going a goal behind – we always believed we could score more goals than the opposition.

'That is the attitude we must apply again.'

Well said, Denis.

Happy retirement – and thanks for all your own particular brand of entertainment.

For the record: Law was with four clubs in his life at the top. He joined Huddersfield Town straight from school in Aberdeen in 1957. Three years later he moved to Manchester City for £55 000, a record at the time. In 1961 Law moved to Turin and teamed up with former Hibs star Joe Baker. He lasted a year and in the summer of 1962 he was signed by Sir Matt Busby for Manchester United. These were his glory years, and at Old Trafford he won two League Championship medals and an English cup badge. He went back to Manchester City, his last club, on a free transfer.

DRAMA IN EUROPE
Inches from disaster, by Andy Rolland, Dundee United F.C.

If you think European football is all glamour and glory, you should have been with Dundee United on their two Cup Winners' Cup trips last season.

For, while I accept that these trips into Europe can take you to such well-known soccer hot-spots as Milan and Madrid, we were not nearly so lucky. In fact, we twice ventured into the deep backwoods of football.

We qualified for the tournament by finishing as runners-up to Celtic in the previous season's Scottish Cup Final — and there was one particular moment when most of us wished we hadn't.

That was one a mist-shrouded Rumanian road en route to Petrosani for the second leg of our first round tie against the local mining team, Jiul.

We almost didn't make it. As our ancient coach came downhill on a mountain road it suddenly went into an uncontrollable skid, swaying dangerously from side to side.

Finally, it left the road completely but, fortunately for the party of 26 players, officials and pressmen, we stopped in a ditch. A few inches more and we would have certainly turned over and, if we had gone off the other side of the road, we would have turned over . . . and gone on turning over until we finished in a river 500 yards away down the hillside.

It was next morning before we were able to joke about that little escape but it wasn't so funny when we discovered that the coach's types were all as bald as a well-known TV detective's head — and that the same coach was taking us the 350 miles back to Bucharest after the game. And it would be dark then!

So I prefer to think that's why Dundee United didn't do too much to impress the 25 000 locals who crammed into the Petrosani Stadium that October afternoon.

They had declared a local holiday in the town so that as many as possible could watch their first ever European tie. Those who didn't have a ticket climbed trees or swarmed on to the roofs of houses overlooking the ground.

And for a time it looked as if they would have something to celebrate. We had won the first leg 3—0 at Tannadice with goals from Davie Narey, Jackie Copland and Pat Gardner but, by the 29th minute, our lead had been cut to just one goal . . . and the Rumanians were howling for more goals and our blood.

But manager Jim McLean brought on Tommy Traynor at the start of the second half and his clever running and possession took all the pressure off United. We got through 3—2 on aggregate.

I did learn one thing to my advantage on that trip to Rumania, that Eastern European food didn't agree with me too well and that there were many things we are used to that just aren't available there.

Andy Rolland, versatile Dundee United star.

Andy Rolland's a great back — but he can also score goals — like this one, against Arbroath.

So, when we were drawn against Bursaspor, of Turkey, in round two, I decided to go prepared. I left Scotland with my usual case, my boots . . . and a food parcel containing chocolate, biscuits, cheese, coffee and tea bags.

Again the first leg of the tie was at Tannadice but, on this occasion, we were unable to build up a lead of any sort. We might have had two or three goals in the first 10 minutes of the tie but, the longer it went, the more confident the Turks became. The match finished in a disappointing goalless draw.

Still, we rated them a poorer side than Jiul Petrosani and gave ourselves a good chance of reaching the quarterfinals despite the poor result at home.

In the event, we didn't play well, again in front of a noisy crowd. They were still a bad side but they got through 1—0 thanks to one of the finest goals I have ever seen, a 25 yard volley by midfield player Vahit that ripped into the net.

Those Turks certainly knew how to celebrate. The referee had to drag half their team back on to the park after they chased the goal-scorer in a lap of honour that ended with himself throwing himself to the ground to give thanks to Allah.

But I'll never be convinced that we lost that tie in the Ataturk Stadium. We lost it at Tannadice and went on losing it as soon as we stepped off the plane in Istanbul.

Turkey may never produce champion footballers but they certainly do a good line in psychological warfare. Where we had experienced bus trouble in Rumania our Turkish trip was plagued by hotel trouble, all, I am certain, skilfully arranged in advance.

Somehow, mysteriously, the cable from our London travel agents confirming our booking at Bursa's best hotel had 'never arrived' and we were shipped off to a sleazy one-star downtown joint.

There we not only had hot and cold running water but huge red beetles running around our rooms. It wasn't for us. We walked out and returned to the top hotel even though we had to sleep three to a room.

The Turks were full of apologies but we knew they had won their point when we were told that even those rooms would not remain available for the second night of our stay we were forced to return downtown – beetles and all.

It wouldn't have been so bad if we had collected a winning bonus but we didn't even manage that against a team that honestly shouldn't have been able to live with us.

So you see, European tournaments are not all that they are cracked up to be at times. Just ask the Dundee United directors. At the end of the day, they were around £5000 out of pocket on the deal.

However, I am not knocking all European football, I know the fans enjoy these games against unusual opponents and they always produce a special atmosphere So I'LL be ready for our next trip abroad. I am saving chocolate and coffee already.

I AM THE HAPPIEST PART-TIMER
by Jimmy Bone, Arbroath F.C.

It has been suggested at various times in the last year or two that many Scottish clubs will soon cut down on full-time players because of the economics of modern football.

That may, in fact, be the case, but I certainly don't agree that an increase in part-time football will necessarily lead to a deterioration in our playing standards.

Because, for me at least, part-time soccer has brought greater satisfaction in the last few years. And, maybe few people realise that I wasn't having my first taste of part-time football when I joined Arbroath last season.

When I first signed for Partick Thistle it was as a part-timer and, although I did become a full-timer for a spell at Firhill, I had reverted to part-time football before I moved to Norwich in 1972.

And, although I was reasonably happy with life in England both with Norwich and Sheffield United and then, on my return to Scotland, with Celtic, going part-time again with Arbroath was no great hardship.

For me, part-time football means far less pressures because I never really felt at ease as a seven-day-a-week soccer player.

Having said that, I have to admit that full-timers do have one major advantage. That is in pre-season training. I honestly feel every player needs a couple of hard weeks of intensive training before the start of each season. Apart from that I see no real disadvantages in mixing football with a job on the outside.

I want you to understand that this is purely a personal view of life as a footballer and that I don't expect a 100 per cent favourable response from fellow professionals.

And neither am I knocking full-time football out of sight. For some of the best moments of my career came as a full-timer, particularly at Norwich.

I enjoyed the training routine at Carrow Road and I know that my play benefitted for a time as a result.

It was there that I earned a fabulous trip with Scotland to the mini-World Cup in Brazil and it was there that I won a full international honour in the World Cup qualifying tie against Denmark in Copenhagen.

And, although I slipped out of the Scotland pool later, I did score one of our goals that night in Denmark in the 4—1 victory that set us on the way to the Finals in West Germany.

So I am entitled to feel I did achieve something at international level as well as winning a League Cup medal with Partick in 1970.

But, while I enjoyed these moments in my career, I did find full-time football a bit of a rat-race at times and I am certainly happy with part-time football at Gayfield.

All right, I know I didn't jump at the chance of signing for Arbroath when manager Albert Henderson made his first approach to Celtic last season.

After all, moving from the premier club in the country to one of the least fashionable took a bit of consideration.

I said No to their original offer but, when they came again later in the season and I had a long chat with the boss I changed my mind.

Mr Henderson impressed me with his ideas and ambitions and, at that particular time, I was stuck fairly permanently in the Celtic Reserve side.

I had scored 21 goals for Celtic that season – but 20 of them had come in the second team. So, the longer I talked to Mr Henderson the more attractive the move became.

And I haven't regretted it. I got a goal

Jimmy Bone, dashing striker.

in my debut against Dundee at Gayfield and the goals continued to come for me in the remaining games of the season.

I know the Gayfield manager is on record as saying Arbroath might well have made it into the Premier League if I had joined them when they made their first approach to Celtic.

That may be the case but I don't think any great harm has been done by our failure to make it into the Top 10.

For one thing, I don't think the new set-up will provide the answers to all the problems of football in Scotland.

Also, I don't believe Arbroath are quite ready for the Premier Division.

I certainly see no harm in the club spending a season or two in a lower Division while some of the younger players at Gayfield gain experience.

These lads need a taste of success to make real progress in the game and I think they have a better chance of achieving this in the new First Division.

And, while I go on looking for goals, I hope I can teach the youngsters at Gayfield a thing or two about the game.

Of course, I am not the only experienced player with the club. Dave Smith, who was appointed player-coach during last season, was a tremendous help to the young lads, before he left the club, because of his great ability to read the game.

Andy Penman and Gordon Marshall, too, are vastly experienced at all levels and I would like to think that we can make a real go of it at Gayfield. We may have slipped out of the glamour set-up at the moment but there is no reason why we shouldn't climb back.

And, what I like most about Arbroath, we'll try to do it by playing attractive football. . . .

Dave Smith, the former Ranger who is showing Arbroath youngsters just how soccer should be played.

WHEN MY SEASON STARTED AT CHRISTMAS: by Gordon Wallace, Dundee F.C.

On the first Saturday of last season I should have been taking the field at Palmerston Park for Dundee's Drybrough Cup tie against Queen of the South.

Instead, I was lying in bed at my Broughty Ferry home thinking how crazy this game we all love can sometimes be.

For, just three days before the start of the new season – the day every player feels he is starting off on a fresh footing – I broke my leg in a training accident.

And, while my team-mates were boarding the coach to take them to Dumfries, I was lying with my leg in a plaster cast. And I had been told that the new season wouldn't start for me until at least Christmas.

That wasn't easy to take, not with the sun streaming through the bedroom window and the warmth making me sweat and itch under the plaster.

But there wasn't anything I could do to change my bad luck and, anyway, I soon learned that it wasn't the end of the world.

In fact, I quickly found that I had more friends in the game than I had ever imagined. I seemed to have someone at the door every other minute of the day and the postman went on overtime for a while.

I was grateful for all the messages of encouragement but the one I remember best came from Bobby Street, the young Aberdeen player who broke his leg twice

right at the start of a promising career.

They all helped buck me up at that particular time but the news that really worked wonders came when I was told that it was a clean break and that I shouldn't have any trouble when the fracture mended.

That's the way it worked out, too, and I was able to start training and eventually make my comeback in the reserves 19 weeks after the break.

I celebrated my return by scoring in my first comeback game and from then on the only thing that delayed my return to the first team was the weather.

Everyone was complaining about the rain and mud around that time but I

Gordon Wallace with his front-line Dundee partner, Jocky Scott.
How times – and styles – change! This picture was taken in 1968 – and shows Gordon Wallace, then with Raith Rovers, being awarded the Scottish Football Writers' Association's Player of the Year Trophy.

Others in the group are former winners of the award – Billy McNeill and Ronnie Simpson of Celtic and John Greig of Rangers.

Hair was shorter then, suit lapels narrower – but there was plenty of skill around.

Gordon Wallace made history that year. He became the fourth player to win the Player of the Year trophy – and broke an Old Firm monopoly. Gordon scored 30 goals and helped Rovers escape relegation.

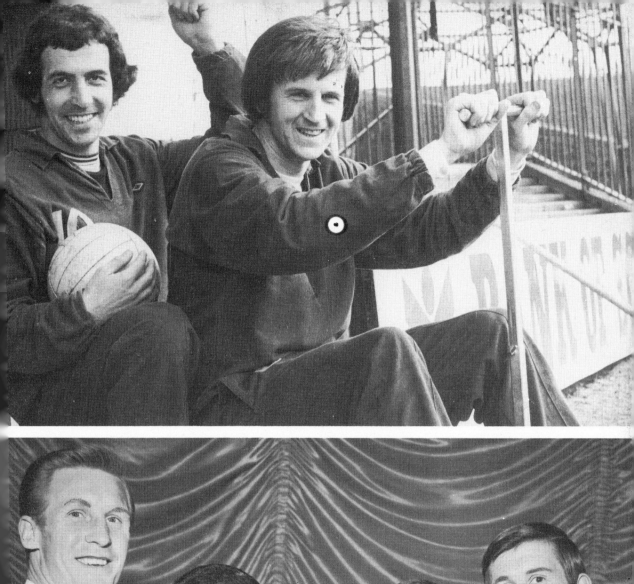

reckoned I had more justification than most. Here I was desperate for match practice and one after another matches were postponed because grounds were unplayable.

But, in the last game of 1974, I came on as substitute against Airdrie in my first appearance of the season for the first team.

And, a few days later, I knew I had come back all the way when, I cracked in our opening goal in the 2—0 win over Dundee United in the New Year derby game.

Although I still felt short of complete fitness it was great to be back and, happily, my return coincided with Dundee hitting something like their true form, though I am not claiming too much of the credit for that.

I reckon making a successful comeback pleased me almost as much as the two other highlights of a career that has brought me tremendous satisfaction.

The first was while I played with Raith Rovers in 1967. At the turn of the year, the halfway stage in the League programme, there seemed nothing could save us from relegation to the Second Division.

Stirling Albion were below us but we were five points behind the third bottom club. The critics, quite rightly, had written us off.

But suddenly things started to happen for the team, and for me in particular. We began to win games and I began on the best scoring streak of my life.

I hit 12 goals in one spell of six matches, including a couple of hat-tricks and by the end of the season we had done just enough to stay in the First Division. I finished with 30 goals.

You can imagine my delight when, as our fate became clear, I received a telephone call from the Football Writers' Association telling me I was about to be named Scotland's player of the year and would I accept the honour.

It was one of the proudest moments of my life as I accepted the trophy, although it was also one of the most nerve-racking. But I did remember to thank my team-mates for all the help they had given me. They shared in the honour, too.

I am pleased to say that I get an invitation to the Player of the Year dinner each Spring as a past winner and I wouldn't miss it for anything. For me it is always one of the highlights of the year.

The other moment I shall always remember was the 1973 League Cup Final on a day of slush and sleet at Hampden when I scored the only goal against Celtic.

We hadn't played particularly brilliantly in the League Cup that year but we did manage to stay the course. And we did play really well despite the shocking conditions that December afternoon.

Dundee might easily have scored a couple of goals early in the game but eventually, in the second-half, I got a chance to shoot on the turn and saw the ball finish in the corner of the net.

Like every other Scottish player, I had dreamed of scoring in an important game at Hampden. The fact that my goal proved to be a winner was a perfect bonus.

And it wasn't a bad moment to keep recalling when things weren't going quite so well while I was out of action with that broken leg.

Dundee have another shooting star to help Gordon Wallace. He's Bobby Hutchison, giving Rangers' keeper Stewart Kennedy no chance with this shot in a game at Dens Park.

DALGLISH - The dream destroyer: Brave Airdrie fail in Cup Final

Scotland had never staged a more intriguing Cup Final. In the one half, Celtic, the fallen champions, out of touch, worried – but still a proud side, a side the bookmakers held as hot favourites. In the other, part-time Airdrie a Cinderella team who had captured the imagination of the neutrals with competent, brave displays, and who had boosted their hopes of Hampden victory with an epic 1—0 win over Rangers at the Ibrox gala day to celebrate the arrival of the League flag the previous Staurday.

No wonder on the bright Saturday afternoon of May 3, 1975, a crowd of 75 457 turned up to see the final.

Airdrie brought plenty of loyal fans from Lanarkshire and while the little Broomfield club could boast of few honours in the game – apart from the day in 1924 when they beat Hibernian 2—0 to take the Scottish Cup for the only time in their long history – they had figured in historic soccer incidents.

In 1871 when the famous Queen's Park visited Airdrie to play the then quaintly named Airdrie Hammer Drivers, the home team had stretched a tape across the top of the posts. Queen's took exception to this and refused to play. After a heated argument, a compromise was reached – the first half was to be played with the posts only, as was the custom then, the second half with the tape in use.

Later, Queen's Park admitted the advantages of the innovation and installed wooden crossbars on their own ground shortly afterwards.

And Airdrie claim that it was on their old Mavisbank ground that the first penalty kick was taken. On June 6, 1891, three days after the general meeting of the SFA had approved the penalty kick law Airdrie played Royal Albert in the Airdrie Charity Cup Final.

It was a match of no great importance until Andrew Mitchell of Airdrie was alleged to have handled the ball and the referee awarded Royal Albert the first penalty kick. And McLuggage of Royal Albert scored – to make a niche for himself in history.

Apart from these incidents and a purple patch in the early 1920s when they not only won the cup but finished runners up in the First Division four times in succession, Airdrie have struggled to survive.

But everyone in football wished them well against Celtic, except, of course, the Celtic fans. For Airdrie are a friendly club and there was sympathy with a team whose players were part-timers, a collection of tradesmen, schoolteachers, labourers and fitters.

And if among them were none with the style or glamour of such Airdrie immortals as Hughie Gallacher, Jock Ewart or Bob McPhail, they were managed by one of Scotland's all-time stars, Ian McMillan and they had found new faith in themselves. They had also beaten

It's an old familiar pose — it shows skipper Billy McNeill in yet another moment of Celtic triumph. He's holding aloft the Scottish Cup won when Airdrie were beaten 3—1 at Hampden.

But it's also a sad picture. It's a picture of Billy saying goodbye to soccer. Just after the final McNeill announced that he was retiring. Few players can have chosen such a dramatic or triumphant moment to say farewell. But it was fitting that McNeill, one of the all-time greats of Scotland and Celtic, a centre-half superb, stepped out when still at the top.

Celtic in the League and scored a double over Rangers. They did not lack confidence, these lads in the red diamond shirts of Broomfield.

Neither, of course, did Celtic. And how determined they were, the team who had already won two trophies, the Drybrough and the League Cups, but who had failed to win the First Division championship for an amazing ten times in a row.

Most determined of all was skipper Billy McNeill, who was to announce after the game that he was retiring from the game to which he had given such illustrious service.

Billy wanted a record – his seventh winner's medal, something no player had ever done with one club, although Bob McPhail and Jimmy McMenemy had picked up that total, with different clubs.

It was the captain's sixteenth cup final, including replays, and a win for Celtic would be a record for the club, their 24th Scottish Cup triumph.

Although Celtic had lost much distinction since the New Year, they had done well in the cup, beating quality teams like Dundee and Hibs and manager Jock Stein had no doubt about the outcome.

'Celtic will win,' he said serenely.

Hampden was at its best for the big game and the teams lined up like this:

Airdrie: McWilliams, Jonquin, Cowan, Menzies, Black, Whiteford, McCann, Walker, McCulloch, Lapsley, Wilson. Subs: March, Reynolds.

Celtic: Latchford, McGrain, Lynch, Murray, McNeill, McCluskey, Hood, Glavin, Dalglish, Lennox, Wilson. Subs: MacDonald, Callaghan.

Referee: I. M. D. Foote, Glasgow.

What a tremendous battle the final turned out to be, perhaps not an epic, not a classic, not a feast of polished football – but there was no lack of drama or excitement.

Airdrie put up a great show and they provided an attractive contest.

At the start, it looked as though Celtic's pace would be too much for the part-time braves of Broomfield. Paul Wilson was racing on the right and Lennox was causing havoc on the left, with Ken Dalglish at the height of his miraculous powers in the centre, giving his marker, John Menzies a harrowing time.

Then Airdrie recovered. They had been given a chasing but suddenly they broke away and it was as well for Celtic, not too

clever in defence during recent matches, that the big Englishman, Peter Latchford, pounced at just the right time to save.

But Dalglish could not be contained. And in 14 minutes it was his artistry that brought the opening and vital goal. It was, indeed, the goal which killed Airdrie's hopes. For one had felt that if the part-timers could have held out for half an hour they could really worry Celtic. Alas, it wasn't to be. . . .

Dalglish combined with his Scotland team colleague, Danny McGrain, to tear the Airdrie defence into tiny pieces. Finally, over came a cross from Dalglish of such accuracy that many Celtic fans swore that he aimed it at Wilson's head. Anyhow, Paul was all on his own to score with a deft if easy header.

Play grew more hectic and there were rough moments as McCulloch and Lapsley fought back bravely in a bid to upset the Celtic defence and Pat McCluskey got himself over hotly involved in keeping them out and was cautioned for a foul.

Although Celtic appeared to have the match well in hand, there were still times when their defence was suspect and they were shaken in the 27th minute when, with the green and white shirts in a tangle, McCulloch's header beat Latchford, only to strike a post. Lapsley, close in, swung recklessly at the rebound, the ball soared over and the young Airdrie player hung his head and cursed his inexperience.

In the 42nd minute, however, Airdrie set the game alight again. They had stuck gallantly to their task and their perseverance paid off. Again the Celtic defenders were not blameless. They failed

Moment of joy for Airdrie in the Scottish Cup Final. The players are congratulating Kevin McCann, who scored their only goal.

This was the goal which killed all Airdrie's Cup Final hopes. It's a penalty, coolly scored by Celtic's Pat McCluskey, giving Airdrie goalkeeper Davie McWilliams no chance.

This was No 2 for Celtic in the final – a devastating header by Paul Wilson.

Celtic's Andy Lynch had a new role in Celtic's Cup Final triumph. He played magnificently at left-back and here he is in a Hampden duel with Billy McCulloch, of Airdrie.

Look back, you Airdrie fans, in delight. Ian McMillan is seen here on his return from Rangers to re-join his old Broomfield club. He captained the team that day against Hibs, whose captain was John Fraser. Now Ian is earning cheers as one of the best managers in the game.

to clear in a massive Airdrie attack. In a mêlée in front of Latchford, two powerful shots were blocked. Then the ball spun to the slight figure of Kevin McCann, whose shot was a beauty and a goal all the way.

Airdrie players danced with delight, their fans went hysterical with joy – and the Airdrie skies were still the brightest blue when disaster struck two minutes later.

They learned a bitter lesson. Never write off Celtic. Angered by the loss of the goal, Celtic hit back with tremendous power. Lennox won a corner on the left. When the ball came over it was the Airdrie defenders' turn to stand gasping as ace scorer Wilson, no giant, came hurtling in to head venomously into the net.

What a sickener for Airdrie. Another mortal blow.

That was the tonic Celtic needed. They

Star of the cup final was Kenny Dalglish, of Celtic. Hard to stop? You can say that again and here he beats an unorthodox challenge from Hearts defender, Dave Clunie.

were in command when the second half began and almost scored in six minutes. More superb footwork by Dalglish saw the Airdrie defence pierced again. But this time tall 'keeper Davie McWilliams came to Airdrie's rescue.

Celtic's pace was telling, however, and the third goal came in the 53rd minute. The veteran Lennox raced down the left and a frantic Paul Jonquin could only push the speedy winger to the ground in a bid to escape disaster. Penalty! And Pat McCluskey scored from the spot.

Celtic were in the driving seat. Airdrie replaced McCulloch and Lapsley with Reynolds and March and it was a wise substitution.

But nothing could stop rampant Celtic. A crackling Dalglish shot from 25 yards scraped the bar and there were many other anxious moments for Airdrie, whose guts were shown when Derek Whiteford had a good shot well saved by Peter Latchford.

Action was still hot and Danny McGrain of Celtic and Mark Cowan of Airdrie were booked late in the game.

But the final ended with Celtic deservedly winning 3—1 and spoiling Airdrie's dream of glory, thanks mainly to the magic of Dalglish.

No one was happier than goalkeeper Latchford, a controversial figure since joining Celtic but a star of the final. 'I can hardly believe it,' he said. 'Just think of what's happened to me – from playing in the second team with West Bromwich Albion to wining a Cup Final medal at Hampden in less than three months.'

Little Airdrie's hopes had vanished – but they took defeat well. Said manager McMillan: 'It was a good match but Celtic went for the ball all the time. They had pace and their passing was better than ours. Whereas we often gave the ball away, Celtic rarely did. Nevertheless, I was delighted with my team and they never gave up.'

Airdrie, perhaps ran out of luck at the wrong time. They lost goals by leaving Wilson unmarked – and they didn't have many smiles from fortune when the Celtic defence blundered.

Celtic, however, were the true and just winners – and Airdrie had no player to match Ken Dalglish, the man with the wondrous touch, the supreme artist in Scotland today.

Probably the saddest contrast was the fact that there could be no doubt that Celtic would go on to achieve more honours – but Airdrie could hardly expect to be back at Hampden quickly.

Yet Airdrie are a great wee club, with everyone pulling together. I wish more wee clubs like Airdrie would believe in themselves, would work as the Broomfield boys do to be allowed to dream of glory even if the prize eludes them at the last minute.

THE BEST BUY IN FOOTBALL

The most fascinating football exercise, even if it is the most futile because there can never be an end product, is that of selecting The Greatest Team That Could Ever Have Played For Scotland.

Fans do it. Players do it. Managers and referees do it. And not so long ago Scotland supremo Willie Ormond did it.

This was the All-time Scottish Eleven the manager named:

Cowan (Morton), Young (Rangers), McNaught (Raith Rovers), Evans (Celtic), Woodburn (Rangers, Baxter (Rangers), Waddell (Rangers), Walker (Hearts), Law (Manchester United), James(Arsenal and Morton (Rangers).

He gave these reasons for his choice: 'I think this team would play well together and that the styles would blend.

Naturally, there were a few murmurs of agreement – and howl after howl of protest. Many felt a galaxy of Scottish talent had been ignored and there is no one as wrathful as a football fanatic whose heroes are excluded from the hall of fame.

And, anyhow, just how good would that team – said blithely by its sponsors to be good enough to give the universe three goals of a start – turn out to be in modern football?

I ask because only a few years ago eighty international football writers from thirty-five countries took part in a poll to select the Best World Eleven during the twenty previous years.

Significantly, not one Scot was included in the selection, which was: Yashin (USSR), Santos (Brazil), Facchetti (Italy), Boszik (Hungary), Wright (England), Beckenbauer (West Germany), Matthews (England), Pele (Brazil), di Stefano (Argentina), Puskas (Hungary), Charlton (England).

These were said to be the pick of the best . . . the elite of the elite.

But would that be the team chosen if the competition were held this season? I doubt it – for undoubtedly the name of **Johan Cruyff**, of Holland, would be included.

And that's why it's such a rash exercise to name the Greatest Ever Team – for new stars are born practically every year. And alleged experts have to be flexible, willing to change their minds. Why, even your old editor has done just that.

A decade ago I picked this as the best team Scotland could have produced, an eleven who could hold up their heads in any company, an eleven of stars:

Cowan, (Morton), Young (Rangers), Cox (Rangers), Evans (Celtic), Meiklejohn (Rangers), McMullan (Manchester City), Waddell (Rangers), Mason (Third Lanark), Gallacher (Newcastle United), James (Preston North End), Morton (Rangers).

That would have been a super side. But as football has progressed and many of those players were not in action during the previous twenty years, I changed my tune.

I chose a team from the past twenty years whose players could stand up to modern pressures, who could sublimate their individual skills to the good of the team and who would not be lost in what is sometimes a soccer jungle euphemistically described as 'modern professionalism', a term which loosely covers a multitude of fouls, jabs, pushes, shoves, kicks and other illegal tactics.

My last team, selected in 1970, was:
Brown (Spurs), Parker (Falkirk), Gemmell (Celtic), Bremner (Leeds), Woodburn (Rangers), Baxter (Rangers), Johnstone (Celtic), White (Spurs), Reilly (Hibs), Steel (Dundee) and Hughes (Celtic).

This team, I believed, would have blended superbly, would have been tough as well as talented.

You'll have observed that many of the players Willie Ormond chose figure in my selections. And Ormond's reasons for his choice are similar to mine. For instance, of his half-back line of Evans, Woodburn and Baxter, he says: 'Evans was the dynamo, Woodburn the stopper, and Baxter the genius, a law unto himself.'

So with my half-back lines: Evans, Meiklejohn, McMullan – Ormond's words apply . . . Bremner, Woodburn, Baxter – you can say these things again.

Yet the big question still hovers: Just how should you go about picking the greatest team? Should you pin your faith in wonderful artists – would star quality be the only qualification?

Or would you try to blend your team? I go for blend.

I also go for players of inspiration, who had power as well as artistry, who could bully, cajole, encourage, who were a team all on their own.

Which brings me to another fascinating, if again futile, soccer puzzle: If you were a manager, who was – or is – the player you would most like to have in your side?

Thousands will say at once: Cruyff. Others might fancy Beckenbauer. Veterans would go for Morton, James, Jackson or Gallacher. Other eyes would light up at the thought of securing Billy Steel or Denis Law or Kenny Dalglish.

To my mind, the greatest buy ever made was of a player who doesn't figure in any Greatest Scottish Elevens – but who will never be forgotten by the fans of one of England's top sides, Tottenham Hotspur.

And if there were a new Davie Mackay available today you can bet that every rich club south of the border would be clamouring for his transfer.

Mackay, now manager of Derby County, combined the best of the two football worlds – the power play, the scientific side.

It has always been my view that power play is just as much traditional Scottish style as the sweet-passing, velvet-gloved game. Mackay was a power player. He also had rare skill. The perfect blend.

He was robust, tackled with the

Was Davie Mackay, former Scotland, Hearts and Spurs wing-half, and now manager of Derby County, the best buy in football?

Many experts believe he was. And certainly Mackay had everything.

THEN – Mackay a decade and more ago. As a Hearts player he received the Footballer of the Year trophy in Edinburgh.

NOW – Mr Mackay, manager of Derby County.

MOMENT OF AGONY for Dave Mackay. In 1964, as you see here, his leg was broken for the second time in nine months. But the brave Mackay made a comeback.

fervour of a knight at a joust, spared no effort, covered every inch of the pitch.

And while no one would ever say he was a suave Jim Baxter, he could play perfect football – making better use than anyone except John White of the open space.

He used to pass the ball – and at once ran on, bawling for the return.

Mackay was a manager's dream – and would be today as well.

I have no doubt that the best buy in football is a brilliant midfield man, wing-half or inside-forward, what's the difference? Much as I adore the skills of a winger, the acrobatics of a goal-keeper, the thrusts of a centre-forward, these players are inclined, in the long run, to be luxuries.

The man who keeps a side plugging along, who cannot afford to be petted, to have off-days, who is eager for the fray Saturday after Saturday, is usually the midfield man. The half-back line, now the midfield masters, is the nerve-centre of the football equipage.

Away back in the early 1900s it was recognized that the half-back was king. Of a famous craftsman of the middle, Kelly Houlter of Blackburn Rovers, it was written:

'To see Houlter stripped for the conflict is to see a mettled steed frolicking for the race or a war-horse snorting for the battle. He is quick, quick as a terrier. He is fast, fast as a hare. He is neat and skilled with his feet as a clog dancer as accurate in his judgement as the Lord High Chancellor, and is in several places – or so it seems – at once. He is as agile as a flea and as difficult to catch. He directs the storm with a subtle brain. In the fire and heat of the game he becomes the embodiment of perpetual motion.'

You could say that of Davie Mackay.

Is there a new Mackay around today?

If there is, he would, I feel, make even the fabulous Cruyff second favourite in any race for a transfer – to an English club, at least.

And how much more would he cost than the £30 000 Spurs paid Hearts for Davie Mackay in 1959.

THEY'RE ON THE SPOT... and seldom spot on

It looked like a save in a million.

The crowd at Fir Park in December 1974 had tensed. Hearts goalkeeper Jim Cruikshank rubbed his hands, watched carefully as Motherwell's John Goldthorp placed the ball on the penalty spot.

Calmly, Goldthorp turned, ran to the ball, hammered it viciously and accurately to Cruickshank's left post.

But there was the 'keeper flying through the air, making contact with the ball that was a blur and turning it away to safety.

The Motherwell crowd sighed. Hearts' colleagues patted the 'keeper on the back. Once again Cruikshank had been the hero of a gallant penalty save.

But Motherwell players weren't convinced that it had been a great save.

They felt Cruikshank had moved long before the penalty kick was taken – and that the kick should have been re-taken.

On the other hand, it could be argued that the 'keeper had guessed right. If he had dived the other way, he would have looked silly. And if Goldthorp had seen the keeper moving he could surely have hesitated – and hit the ball the other way.

Which, of course, is not the point. Law 14 says clearly: 'The opposing goalkeeper must stand (without moving his feet) on his own goal-line between the goal-posts until the ball is kicked.'

In recent years, however, the law has been broken time after time. The 'keeper moves – and the referee takes no action if a save is made. For instance, Spanish goalkeeper Iribar obviously moved yards long before Tom Hutchison took the vital penalty for Scotland against Spain in the European Championship game at Hampden – and saved the kick.

Let me blunt. Goalkeepers have always moved. Yet today more and more penalties are being missed. Why? Where have all the penalty experts gone, men like Rangers' Johnny Hubbard and Kilmarnock's Jock McEwan, who would have kicked themselves silly if they had missed from the spot?

It's true that in the old days penalties were missed – but not many and certainly not half as many as are missed nowadays.

As goalkeepers seem in with a real hope in the one-against-one situation, we wonder if we are in an age of super goalkeepers or an age in which referees don't do their duty in watching the goalies' feet.

One reason for the 'keepers' success is television. The cameras reveal the kickers' secrets and clubs watch carefully to see to which side of the goal the spot aces like to aim.

Overleaf:

How it should be done! Don't tell Celtic fans some of their players can't take penalties. Here wee Jimmy Johnstone blasts his shot high into the net from the spot – and it's the penalty that won the Drybrough Cup for Celtic for the first time.

So today's top penalty scorers vary their kicks. Says Sandy Jardine of Rangers: 'You've just got to vary your method because 'keepers have been watching how you do it on telly.

'Mind you, I don't blame the goalie for moving fast, if he can get away with it. He has a lonely job and really at penalty kicks I find it's the outfield players who try to talk you out of scoring by chattering as you're about to take the kick.'

'Keepers, however, do cheat. 'Always have, always will,' says Jimmy Brown cheerfully. And Jimmy should know. The burly former Hearts, Kilmarnock and St Mirren goalkeeper was one of the best of all time and there's nothing about keeping that he doesn't know.

Now retired and an Ayrshire business-man, Jimmy feels goalies get away with moving much more than they used to. 'Referees don't seem to worry so much now,' he said, 'and 'keepers take advantage of that fact.'

It's Jimmy's view that no goalkeeper has ever saved a well-taken penalty legally. But he points out that 'keepers can also move the wrong way and it's not often that, if he doesn't move, the ball has been kicked straight at him.

'Keepers wouldn't have a prayer unless they moved. They've done nothing to lose. Most people don't expect a goalie to save a penalty — so it's a bonus if he does.

Nevertheless, ace penalty kickers are hard to find these days. For the man on the spot must be nerveless and com-pletely oblivious to all that's going on around him — and plenty is, what with backchat and wisecracks.

Wee Johnny Hubbard seemed in a world of his own as he trotted up to the ball, shimmied, sent the 'keeper the wrong way and accurately placed the ball in the net.

Everyone had complete confidence in Johnny, felt assured he would score. It's different today and good penalty-takers are scarcer than consistent Scotland international teams.

What's the best way to take a penalty? Some prefer the Hubbard method. Others think that Tommy Gem-mell of Celtic and Dundee was the best at the job, lashing the ball fiercely into the top of the net.

The real secret, I feel, is to hit the ball to a corner. It must be accurate — and accuracy counts more than pace, although the ball must be reasonably well struck.

What about the poor old referee? Is he the villain of the piece when he fails to spot a 'keeper moving?

Referees are really up against it, for it's a split-second matter. Their eyes can't be in two places at once.

After all, goalkeepers have become the greatest gamblers in soccer and that's why they're enjoying a winning streak. The referee has also to watch that other players don't encroach on the penalty area.

And it's not easy to detect on the field that the 'keeper has moved before the kick has been taken if your eyes are elsewhere.

I'm for the 'keeper. They are now fully prepared to commit themselves and

Tommy Gemmell, of Celtic and Dundee, knew the right way to take penalties — blast the ball viciously past the opposing 'keeper.

Some referees may allow goalkeepers to move — but not top whistler Bobby Davidson, one of the best in the world.

An expert spot-kicker is Sandy Jardine of Rangers. Here he gives young Ayr United 'keeper Ian McGiffen no chance with this penalty taken at Ibrox.

82

consequently can achieve the seemingly impossible.

Other factors are also involved in this controversy. 'Keepers' techniques have improved out of all recognition, which is one reason there are fewer goals in the game today.

And, as Sandy Jardine pointed out, too many kickers are so predictable in their method that 'keepers are tipped off and get the heroic result.

Anyhow, in the old days 'keepers were allowed to move if they wanted to.

The penalty-kick law was passed at a meeting of the International Board in Glasgow on 2 June, 1891, following a proposal by the Irish FA.

It became Law 13 (not 14 as now) and stated: 'If any player shall intentionally trip or hold or push an opposing player, or wilfully handle the ball, within twelve yards from his own goal-line, the referee shall, on appeal, award the opposing side a penalty kick, to be taken from any point twelve yards from the goal-line, under the following conditions:

'All players, with the exception of the player taking the penalty kick, and the goalkeeper (who shall not advance more than six yards from the goal-line) shall stand at least six yards behind the ball. The ball shall be in play when the kick is taken and a goal may be scored from the penalty kick, but the ball shall not be again played by the kicker until it has been played by another player. If necessary, time of play shall be extended to admit of the penalty kick being taken.'

And in a booklet of hints to referees, issued by the SFA in 1893, it was said of penalties:

'I would just specially mention that, no matter where the intentional "trip hold, or handle" takes place within the twelve-yards line, even although it should be under the bar, the ball must be taken back to the twelve-yard line and kicked from any point on it the kicker chooses, all opponents, except the goalkeeper, being six yards behind him.'

I wonder what Douglas Dick would think of present-day penalty-kick takers. A chairman of Kilmarnock FC, Douglas was a star with Morton, Rangers, Liverpool and Third Lanark. And he scored the first penalty in Scottish League football on 4 August 1891. He was playing for Morton against Celtic. The referee twice enforced the new Law 13. The first was in favour of Morton and Douglas scored easily, despite the advancing goalie.

'Keepers did all they could in the old days to distract the kicker. But it wasn't until season 1929–30 that the penalty law, making it compulsory for a goalkeeper to stand still on his own goal-line until the ball is kicked came into operation.

Compulsory?

Don't make the present-day spot-kickers laugh!

THE FASCINATING FOOTBALL QUIZ

Here it is again – the toughest football quiz of all.

It's the quiz which separates the men from the boys, it's the unusual quiz, the quiz that proves whether you know the game inside out or not.

It is, in short, the quiz for the superior fan.

Can you argue with the referee about the rules – and be proved right?

Is your memory top-class?

Are you really an expert on our wonderful game?

Here's your chance to show your skill.

BEAT THE REFEREE!

1—The centre-forward hits a terrific shot. The 'keeper has no chance. It's a goal all the way. You, the referee, have no doubt. You award a goal. Suddenly there's a protest from the goalkeeper. 'Hey, Ref,' he says, 'the ball's burst, so it can't be a goal.' You ignore the appeal and allow the goal to stand. Are you right?

2—The second half just started, a quick raid by Rangers – and Parlane has the ball in the net. No infringement that you as the referee can see. So you give a goal. But Celtic protest. Their goal-keeper has forgotten his gloves. He ran off the field to get them. You didn't notice his absence. Now that it's been brought to your attention you disallow the goal. Did you make the correct decision?

3—The wee winger takes a corner. The ball hits a post and comes right back to him. Then the winger shoots the ball into the net. You give a goal. Are you right?

4—The little ball boy was Albion daft. He just loved that team. So when a penalty kick was awarded against them, unjustly in the lad's view, he felt he had to do something. He certainly did. When the opposing centre-forward was about to take the penalty, the boy was right behind the goal, jumping, gesticulating, making faces at the penalty-kick taker. The centre-forward was put off his kick and missed. What should you, the referee, do?

5—You are examining the players' boots in the dressing-room before the game. You notice that the goalkeeper is wearing a heavy ring. So you ask him to take it off. 'Sorry ref,' says the 'keeper, 'I can't. It's stuck and it won't come off.' 'I'm sorry, too,' you say, 'but you can't take part in the game as that ring is dangerous and could cause injury to opponents.' Were you right?

6—You are becoming exasperated with a goalkeeper who is facing a penalty kick. Three times he has moved before the kick is taken. He does it again. You lose your patience and book the 'keeper.

'I'm fed up,' says the goalie and he moves out of the goal and asks the right back to take over. He does so and saves the penalty. But the 'keeper says, 'Well done, pal,' and goes back into goal. Should he be allowed to stay in goal?

7—Both your watches, for some strange reason, have gone wonky. Unfortunately, you play only 42 minutes in the first half – and you don't notice this until the second half has started. How long should you allow for the second half to last?

8—A strange quickie. The ball lands on the bar – and sticks there, by a remote chance – a piece of chewing gum left by the 'keeper. What should you, the referee, do?

SHORT – BUT NOT SO SIMPLE

1—Which Celtic player scored the club's first-ever goal in the European Cup?

2—Who was the oldest player in the Scotland team which played Spain at Hampden in the European Championship match?

3—Who scored Scotland's first-ever goal in the final stages of the World Cup? A clue – it was in Sweden in 1958.

4—Which club did Tommy Hutchison, the Scotland star, play for before joining Coventry City?

5—What senior club played in Stirling before Stirling Albion?

6—Really tough – What was the name of the ground played on by Edinburgh's St Bernard?

7—The great Hughie Gallagher was perhaps Scotland's most famous centreforward. How many different clubs was he with when he played for Scotland?

SPOT THE PLAYERS

1—He turned down a chance to join Rangers. Which was unusual for he was playing with Queen's Park and he was a goalkeeper and at the time the Ibrox club were looking for a new 'keeper. When he decided to turn professional, Rangers moved in – but he went elsewhere.

He had a soft spot for Clyde – but he didn't join them either. But when he joined his new club he wasn't too popular with the fans for he replaced one of their idols, a burly goalie who eventually moved to Liverpool.

He once kept goal for the Glasgow Primary Schools team which won a major award and Alex Willoughby was one of his team-mates. He's reckoned one of the most consistent 'keepers in Britain. Can you name him?

2—He's an Anglo, he is noted as an attacker but he plays in England with a No. 5 shirt. His happiest memories are of playing against two of the greatest teams in football history – and being undefeated. Once against Real Madrid in 1964 and against Brazil in 1966.

He was in Scotland's World Cup squad in Germany – and many experts thought he should have played.

What's his name?

3—He's one of Scotland's most intelligent players, a schemer, a prober, an artist. He has played in England and he was a member of the Scotland squad which went on a glamorous round-the-world tour a few years ago.

He didn't enjoy his stay in England and he was glad to return home and join his former club.

Now he's a popular favourite elsewhere.

Who is he?

DOWN MEMORY LANE

1—There are several famous names in this picture of a British Services team during the war. Among them are Frank Swift and Stanley Matthews. There's also one of the greatest footballing Scots of all time. What's his name?

2—How styles change! Now soccer stars look like pop artists. This player doesn't turn out like this nowadays – but he's still turning out in style. Who is he? And can you name his team-mates running out behind him?

3—Are these the famous Wembley
Wizards?

4—Today this player is a manager. Who is he?

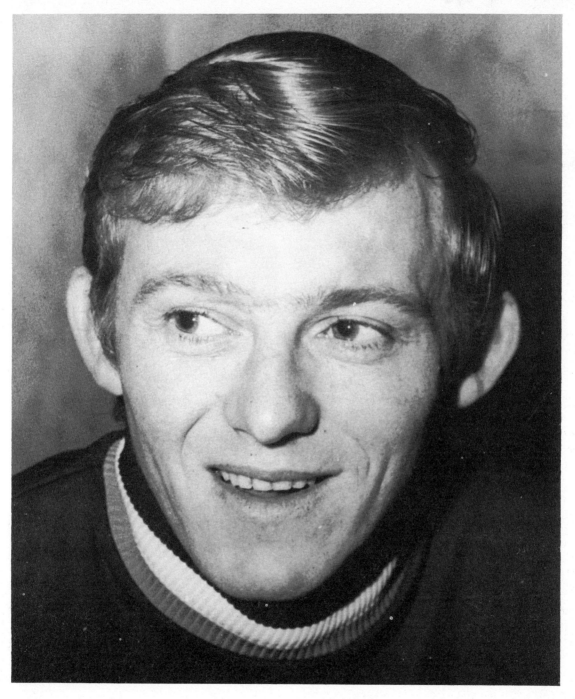

5—Once they were Old Firm rivals. Do you remember them?

6—Of course you remember the face, the name just eludes you. Well, not so long ago he was a splendid player with a Glasgow club. Name, please?

THE ANSWERS

BEAT THE REFEREE

1—No. The ball must have burst before it entered the net and so ceased to be round. You would call for a new ball and restart with a drop.

2—Yes. You would restart the match again. The laws state there must always be a goalkeeper.

3—No. The correct decision is an indirect free kick.

4—The boy should have been removed from behind the goal. Where a goal has not resulted from a penalty due to the kicker being distracted in any way, a re-take should be ordered.

5—Not really. The danger of the ring could have been overcome by covering with cotton wool and a bandage – and, of course, a glove.

6—Yes. If the referee is informed a change of goalkeeper can be carried out any time during the match.

7—Only 45 minutes – plus any injury time.

8—One way would be to ask an attacking player to knock it down and award a free kick against him.

SHORT BUT NOT SO SIMPLE

1—Tommy Gemmell against Zurich in 1966.

2—Billy Bremner.

3—Jimmy Murray, of Hearts, against Yugoslavia.

4—Blackpool.

5—King's Park.

6—The Royal Gymnasium Ground.

7—Airdrie, Newcastle, Chelsea, Derby.

SPOT THE PLAYER

1—Bobby Clark, of Aberdeen.

2—Peter Cormack, of Liverpool.

3—Harry Hood, of Celtic.

DOWN MEMORY LANE

1—Sir Matt Busby, of Manchester United – front row, right.

2—John Greig, followed by Billy Ritchie and Bobby Watson, both with Motherwell.

3—No – this is the Scotland team which played at Hampden in 1929. Among the Wizards of the year before are Hughie Gallacher, Alex Jackson, Jack Harkness, Jimmy McMullan, Alex James and Alan Morton.

4—George Miller, of Dunfermline Athletic.

5—Willie Johnstone (Rangers) and Ian Young (Celtic).

6—Johnny Flanagan, of Partick Thistle.

DANGER! - MEN AT PLAY

. . . BUT can you call soccer play nowadays?

Much of the fun, they say, has gone out of the game, packed with tension, worry, fear.

Sometimes it isn't a sport any more. It's big business, with rewards high, penalties for failure severe.

Nevertheless, you've got to be tough and you must be brave to be a top player today.

For no matter what football is short of, danger isn't one of those commodities.

Big hearts are still needed, there's no time for hesitancy, and players must take a chance.

Danger-men – that's the role of the modern soccer star, as these pictures show:

Even the bravest get hard knocks. Doughty Dundee centre-half George Stewart lies in agony after a clash in a match against Rangers.

Goalkeepers must have the courage of the troopers in the Charge of the Light Brigade. Sometimes theirs is a fearsome as well as fearful job. 'Keepers must brave flying studs, thundering assaults, nasty injury to preserve their charge. Here's an example of real bravery. Ayr United goalkeeper Ally McLean is icicle-cool as he dives at his peril to grasp the ball in an all-out Aberdeen attack.

94

Oh, my head! But there's no thought of injury in the minds of Alex McAnespie and Doug Somner as they go hell-for-leather to head the ball in a Partick Thistle – Ayr United game. You can't flinch and be a soccer ace.

96

Never mind an obstacle – just go for that ball. That's the hallmark of an outstanding attacker. But this time Derek Johnstone of Rangers finds an opponent just as determined as he is to get to the ball first – and Airdrie 'keeper McWilliams wins this joust.

Danger doesn't always come from opponents. Your own colleagues in their anxiety to help can mean a bruise. But it doesn't matter as long as the ball is won. Aberdeen 'keeper Bobby Clark shoves his own centre-half Willie Young out of the way as he clears in a Rangers raid.

Pitches, too, can be dangerous. Never
mind, the surface, though, never mind the ice
and snow and treacherous footing. The
game must go on – as fast as always. And
here's a thrill in the snow during a Celtic –
Dundee United tussle.

OH, COME ON, PLAY THE GAME, YOU CHAPS!

There's always someone bleating. There's always someone moaning that football is dying, that the fun has gone out of the game, that modern tactics stultify soccer.

Where are all the characters nowadays, they demand? Where are the individual artists, the stars who can command crowds all on their own?

Perhaps football isn't as attractive as it once was and those of us who are veterans in the game must be forgiven if we can't always see it through rosy lens for what, whether game, music, film or book, can be as delightful to us as it was in our springtime?

The squeal of the traditionalists is that football has become over-organized. It's being sacrificed on the altar of God Robot, they say, and – It's being played to a formula, and – Numbers mean more than skill, and – Clubs should sign draughtsmen and economics experts instead of footballers.

So we have turned the complete circle. In the old days, the essence of the game was its lack of organization, with teams in different parts of the country playing to their own rules, some of them verging on barbarity, and no one could agree on what were foul tactics and what was fair wear and tear.

Now that the game has been reduced to uniformity there are still complaints.

What we must realize is that the game has always been changing and there were murmurs of discontent when teams stopped playing three centre-forwards, when the W-plan in attack was started (and how many in 1975–6 demand that we return to a five-forward attack?), when the centre-half became a third full back, when passes were made more significant than individual dribbling.

If you think, however, that football has changed all that much in the past two decades or so, just look at these pictures.

They show that football still has humour, still all the human emotions, anger, glee, despondency, error.

Come on, admit it – there's nothing of the robot, nothing of the formula, nothing of what experts call the grey, faceless football of the seventies about these incidents.

What you see is as ageless as the game itself, going back to Billy Bunter's immortal cry: 'Play the game, you cads'.

And even if it wasn't funny at the time to the participants, they must have had a good laugh about it later.

Yes, football is still the sport of the humourist, the sport that makes us grin, makes us feel it's the best in the world.

John Brownlie of Hibs isn't selling the jersey here, although Dixie Deans of Celtic seems to want it very much. And it's short shrift for a sleeve.

If looks could kill . . . No need to tell you how wee Jimmy Johnstone of Celtic is feeling as he lies on the ground after being upended by a Dundee United player.

Hey, mind my ribs, Joe, shouts Celtic's Billy McNeill as Joe Harper of Hibs goes a wee bit near the bone.

Never mind the ballet act, demands Rangers centre-half Colin Jackson as John Blackley of Hibs and Derek Parlane also turn on cute expressions as they go up for a high ball.

Overleaf:

Celtic 'keeper Ally Hunter isn't too pleased with Joe Harper of Hibs, as he tries in vain to get a hand to the ball which the Easter Road striker touched into the net in a League Cup Final.

JOE'S HAT-TRICK BLUES

Hours after the League Cup Final had ended, Hibernian striker Joe Harper still couldn't believe it. 'Imagine it,' he gulped. 'I scored three goals, a hat-trick, in one of the top games of the season – yet we were beaten.'

And everyone who was at Hampden on October 26, 1974, knew Joe had been a hero, a devastating finisher who had scored one of the most notable hat-tricks Scotland's great old ground has ever seen.

The trouble for Hibs was that Celtic's Dixie Deans had also scored three wonderful goals. AND Jimmy Johnstone had netted once. And Paul Wilson. And Steve Murray.

But it was the remarkable Dixie Deans who had really broken Hibs' hearts....

No wonder the Easter Road defenders hated the sight of the alert Celt. The week before the final he had scored three against Hibs in a League game – and in the 1972 Scottish Cup Final he had also made it a three-goal day in Celtic's 6—1 victory over manager Eddie Turnbull's Edinburgh team.

Hibs were on the spot as they travelled to Glasgow for the League Cup Final. They were staggering from two shattering defeats in four days from Celtic and Italy's Juventus in the UEFA Cup.

It was a dismal transformation for Hibs – but not an unusual one, for inconsistency is the bugbear of Easter Road – as only weeks before they had won nationwide praise for brilliant attacking and entertaining performances.

And that was the basis of manager Turnbull's pre-match pep talk: 'You just can't lose that kind of ability overnight,' he told his players. 'Get out on to Hampden and show just how good you are.'

Over at Parkhead, manager Jock Stein was also talking to his players. 'This will be a different match,' he warned them. 'Don't expect another huge victory. Hibs are a good team and they are desperate to make a comeback.'

While the fans, however, expected Celtic to win, there were two important factors which couldn't be overlooked: Hibs surely could never be as bad again as they had been against Celtic and Juventus; and the final was to be contested with the experimental offside law in operation – a law which didn't please Jock Stein.

Celtic started the game hot favourites – but Hibs fans took hope from the fact that in recent League Cup Finals Dundee, Partick Thistle, Hibs and Rangers had all gone in against the Celts as barely quoted under-dogs and came out on top.

On the whole, though, most people imagined ony a miracle could give Hibs victory against a storming Celtic side playing in their eleventh successive League Cup Final.

Wee Joe Harper did his best to

achieve it . . . but three goals just weren't good enough.

Yet, if a great chance had been seized in the opening minutes, it might have been all so different for Hibs.

Only five minutes had gone when an Arthur Duncan cross found Alec Edwards. Celtic fans trembled. Was the League Cup bogey about to strike again?

Not this time. Edwards, usually so calm and efficient, blasted the ball over from ten yards.

And that, really, was that.

In the next minute, Celtic went ahead.

Playing enchanting football, they found the gaps which had been the downfall of the Hibs defence in recent games and carved a splendid goal out of fine ball play.

The sprightly Deans easily beat centre-half Derek Spalding and let Ken Dalglish have the ball. Dalglish, back to top form, coolly waited for the tackle by John Brownlie, then slipped the ball ahead.

Jimmy Johnstone had intelligently raced through the middle and was in the clear to accept the precise pass and stroke the ball into the net.

And so Celtic turned on the style, outclassing forlorn Hibs with football that had star quality, touches of ballet, indeed, with merry Johnstone the star.

Hibs chased shadows — Tricky Johnstone was uncatchable, his passes brilliant. Dalglish was lord of the middle, spreading play beautifuly. Target man Deans, the Hibs' nightmare, despite his lack of inches, won the ball in the air, to the terrible confusion of the defenders.

But Celtic were finding at this stage that it was more difficult to score goals than it had been the previous Saturday. They missed chances and there was commendable bravery in the Easter Road defence despite all the pressure.

Now and again Hibs, a proud team, attacked, with Iain Munro, a strong,

direct runner, and the speedy Duncan matching the Celtic raiders for skill and style.

As the Celtic supporters began to worry after seeing a Murray goal being chalked off — a tight offside decision — and a strong penalty claim turned down, the Parkhead team struck viciously, proving their power and ability to be first to the ball.

In the 34th minute, a fine long pass from Pat McCluskey had the Hibernian defence in a dither and although three of them could have cleared the nippy Deans was first to the ball, despite the attentions of his shadows, and amazingly squeezed the ball past onrushing goalkeeper Jim McArthur.

Then Hibs showed their courage and skill — thanks to Joe Harper. With the contest seemingly over, Joe struck devastatingly three minutes before half-time with a goal to remember. Duncan's corner kick was turned into goal by Pat Stanton, touched on by Alex Cropley — and somehow or other, lethal Harper slammed the ball into the net.

Against the stiff breeze in the second half, Hibs brought on Bobby Smith for John Brownlie — and almost brought off the miracle. Alas, Harper mis-kicked in front of goal and a great chance was lost.

And, as in the first half, Celtic gave thanks for the escape in fine style. They darted straight to the other end to increase their lead. A splendid Murray pass sent Johnstone in. The wee man parted perfectly to Paul Wilson and the outside-left ran on to give McArthur no chance.

Hibs refused to surrender and, just when Celtic were at the height of their

Overleaf:

The goal that started it all. Jimmy Johnstone scores Celtic's first goal against Hibs in the League Cup Final at Hampden.

The goal that amazed everyone. Hibs defenders stare in astonishment as Dixie Deans header cannons into the net.

mastery and about to run away with the trophy, they got a goal back, in the 61st minute.

A cute move saw a mix-up in the Celtic goal. Hunter and McNeill hesitated. And Harper got the credit of putting the ball in the net.

Again, though, Celtic were equal to the stout challenge.

In another three minutes, Deans, showing international class, took a pass from Murray, beat John Blackley and scored with a cracking low drive.

And two minutes later Dixie completed his hat-trick with the most astonishing goal seen at Hampden.

Previous page:

The goal that finished it. Steve Murray gets Celtic's sixth goal.

A Wilson corner reached Johnstone. Jimmy hooked his shot viciously but wide. The ball hit Deans — or, if you like, Dixie met the ball — on the forehead and cannoned, sizzling, past the amazed McArthur.

Hibs replaced Duncan with Willie Murray — and the newcomer was treated almost at once to Celtic's sixth goal. Once again Dalglish made a fine pass and Murray finished with a well-placed shot.

And again Hibs hit back. Certainly they had courage. With seven minutes left, Harper hustled the Celtic defence and squeezed the ball past Hunter from a Munro cross to complete the second hat-trick of the day.

And two minutes later Ally Hunter, another Celt back to top form, had to make an acrobatic save to prevent Joe scoring his fourth goal.

The game finished 6—3 for Celtic.

The goal that gave Hibs hope. Joe Harper squeezes his second past the Celtic defence.

And they had swept aside the memory of four successive League Cup Final failures to win the trophy in superb style.

While Celtic were the better team and while Hibs mourned the loss of 15 goals in a week, the Easter Road side were by no means humiliated and they made the match worthy of its Hampden setting, playing with spirit and no little skill before being overwhelmed by the super champions, at top form and a match for any club in the world.

Deans was the Celtic hero – and he received his reward later by gaining his first international cap against East Germany the following week.

And Joe is convinced Hibs will go places soon.

If only they could be more consistent. . . .

A crowd of 53848 saw the final – and that meant that a huge total of 830672 fans had watched Celtic's eleven successive League Cup finals.

The teams were:

Celtic: Hunter, McGrain, Brogan, Murray, McNeill, McCluskey, Johnstone, Hood, Deans, Dalglish, Wilson. Subs: McDonald, Lennox.

Hibernian: McArthur, Brownlie, Bremner, Stanton, Spalding, Blackley, Edwards, Cropley, Harper, Munro, Duncan. Subs: Smith, Murray.

Referee: J. R. P. Gordon, Newport-on-Tay.

It took wee Joe Harper a long time to recover from the shock of scoring a hat-trick in a final – and losing. But Joe had a fine season.

'Hibs are the best side I have ever played in,' he said, 'and that's no disrespect to Morton, Huddersfield, Aberdeen and Everton.'

The smile that says we've won. It's from Celtic's hat-trick hero Dixie Deans, being congratulated by Steve Murray, another scorer.

The symbol of success. Celtic players with the League Cup after their victory over Hibs.

The toast to success. Celtic's backroom boys fill the League Cup with champagne — Bob Rooney, Jimmy Steele and manager Jock Stein.

FITBA' BELONGS TO GLASGOW:
A tribute to a soccer crazy city

Glasgow is celebrating its 800th anniversary. And although the great old city is famous for shipbuilding, iron founding, its university, the HLI, it has also cause to be proud of what it did for Scottish football.

The city was the centre of the game at its start. Today it has the most famous clubs in the land, Rangers and Celtic.

Glasgow and football – they go hand in hand.

This is our tribute to dear auld Glesca' toon, the home of soccer. . . . Who knows where football was born? The game is a good deal older than our country itself. What we do know is that soccer began to be played in the 1860s. And if the game was originated in England by muscular Christians, young clergymen who played the game at Cambridge and Oxford, there is no doubt that in Scotland the city of Glasgow was instrumental in making it our most popular sport.

Glasgow is still, despite the spread of other, more modern attractions, the most football-crazy city in the world, where news of a soccer star's pulled hamstring muscle is to his club's fans as appalling as the announcement of the outbreak of a third world war.

Glasgow holds the most significant crowd records – the record British attendance, 149547 at Hampden Park to see Scotland play England in 1937, 146433 to watch Aberdeen face Celtic in the 1937 Scottish Cup Final, 127621 at the Hampden European Cup Final of 1960 – to study two foreign teams, mark you, Real Madrid and Eintracht.

Glasgow has the world's fiercest football rivalry – that between the Old Firm of Celtic and Rangers. And today these two are among the most famous footballing clubs in the world.

How did it all start? It began with Queen's Park and if it hadn't been for the founders of the renowned amateur side, it is doubtful if the game would ever have taken the place it has in the world of sport – and it is certain Scotland would not have become the nursery and the home of modern football.

Difficulties at the start were heartbreaking. It was almost impossible, for instance, to find opponents and old Rugby attributes lingered around the new code. Queen's Park were formed in 1867 but it was not until 1872 that handling, carrying and hacking fell into disuse.

For five years Queen's Park made experiments. It was still hard to find opponents but, by studying the game in matches among its own members, Queen's gradually reached perfection and applied for admission to the only governing body then in existence, the Football Association of England.

Queen's made a hit against English sides, assumed the responsibility of playing the first international between Scotland and England, providing all the Scottish players, and fostered the sport in other parts of Scotland. So the men of vision and valour behind Queen's Park made the club famous. It began to prosper. The success of one club against a nation – the first game at Hamilton Crescent in Glasgow had ended in a 0—0 draw – had given an astonishing impetus to football in Scotland. The number of clubs increased rapidly. No longer were Queen's in splendid isolation. They began to find plenty of opposition at home – mainly, of course in the Glasgow area.

What a record Queen's Park, the pride of Glasgow, had at the start! Formed in July 1867 the club did not lose a goal until a Vale of Leven forward scored against them in 1875 and were not defeated until 1876 when their first reverse – by the Wanderers of England – was a national disaster.

Queen's were determined, however to make soccer a national sport, not a monopoly of Hampden. They founded new bodies – and although most of them had their headquarters in Glasgow it was to the Hampden pioneer work that the Edinburgh Association came about.

Queen's of course, were behind the founding of the Scottish Football Association – and then took over the Scottish Cup, with the amazing record of winning the trophy from 1873–4 when the competition started until 1877 when they lost in the final to their arch enemies, Vale of Leven.

Football, however, was progressing – and professionalism came in, much to the disgust of Queen's Park, who remain amateur to this day. A new era was about to start in Scotland – the era of Rangers and Celtic, Glasgow and the country's most powerful clubs. The day of the notable amateurs was really over.

If Queen's were ancient Scottish football history incarnate, Celtic and Rangers are the major figures on the Scottish scene – Glaswegians still.

For nearly 100 years the Old Firm have clashed in Homeric rivalry – and it is generally agreed that their games are the most famous club fixtures in all soccer.

Certainly these two clubs dominated football after the grip of Queen's Park was broken – and Glasgow's supremacy in football, even though, alas, it seems that fewer natives of the city play for the teams, is such that the greatest victory any other Scottish club can have is success over one or other of the Big Two.

If Queen's Park now languish in the Second Division, they can still claim to have the greatest and most famous football stadium in the world. It is not as glamorous as Wembley, where a football match looks like something from a Hollywood epic in Technicolor, with bands playing, sun shining and bright paint glinting. It is not as modernly efficient as Parkhead or Ibrox, where you gain the impression that football is big business.

But Hampden has a majesty and a beauty all its own. To visit Hampden, is to visit a temple. It is as stark, stern and grey as the battlements of a Scottish fort. It is probably at its most impressive on a dull Scottish day of chilly smirr and peevish, snell wind, when the flags bicker angrily and the vast crowd huddles together for comfort.

It is the third playing field of Queen's

What a team! Glasgow went daft about this great Rangers side at the start of the century. They won the Scottish League four times in a row from 1898–99 until 1901–2. You see them here photographed in all their glory after they had won the flag for the third time in succession.

119

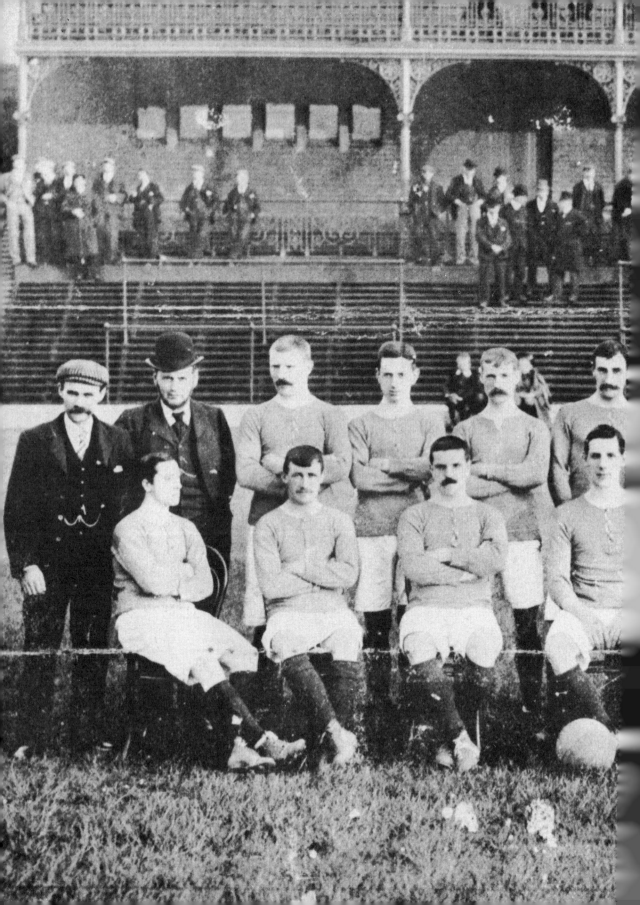

Park, begun in 1899, with work starting on the 'classic slopes' in 1900.

Hampden belongs to Glasgow and has staged practically every game of high importance in Scotland.

Look back, however, and practically everything that made Scottish soccer great started in Glasgow. In a small temperance hotel in Bridge Street the SFA came into being on March 13, 1873. In 1890 the Scottish held their first meeting in Glasgow – with nearly all the clubs being local, Celtic, Rangers, Third Lanark, St Mirren, Hearts, Dumbarton, Abercorn, Cambuslang, Vale of Leven, Cowlairs and Renton.

Today clubs such as Hibs, Hearts, Aberdeen, Dundee, Dundee United, Motherwell, Kilmarnock and Ayr United contribute more than a fair share of football in Scotland.

But to Glasgow goes the honour of introducing the game, fostering it – and keeping it great. Indeed, the pattern of Scottish football is anything but complex, resolving itself simply into the Queen's Park era and then the Rangers–Celtic era.

The city can be proud of the part it has played in football – but then, of course, Glasgow is what football is all about, warm-hearted and tough, often rough, volatile, excitable, and passionate about its principal care – the fitba'.

What was it like away back in the old days in Glasgow when football was getting into its stride?

Equipment was a darned sight cheaper then. In the 1890s you could buy 'The

And Glasgow is still daft about the game. Rangers skipper John Greig salutes the fans at an Ibrox gala day to celebrate their League title victory in 1974–5. A crowd of 63,000 turned up to see Rangers play Airdrie and skipper Greig did a lap of honour in an old-style pony and trap to the delight of the fans.

Holborn' match football for 10s. 6d. and a good quality jersey cost 3s. 7½d. while the 'Referee' football boot could be had for 8s. 11d. A favourite meeting place of the Glasgow football folk was Tom Vallance's Club bar and restaurant in Paisley Road Toll, where you could eat your fill for a shilling.

Reflecting the mood of today, however, was an item in the SFA report for 1892–3 which said: 'Rough play – This unsportsmanlike feature of the game is still prominent but the Committee trust that, by continued punishment and strict refereeing, it may soon become a thing of the past.' Ah, wishful thinking. . . .

The leading sports newspaper was *Scottish Sport* and it cost one penny every Tuesday and Friday. The reporters then wrote about teams unknown today – Cowlairs, Carrington, Carfin Shamrock, Dykehead, Glengowan, United Abstainers, Polton Vale, Smithson Hibs, Orion and Broxburn Shamrock.

Popular then, just as they are today, were the sports snippets at the bottom of the newspaper columns – snippets such as:

'Record 6d. gate – £572 12s. 3d. was drawn at the gate and £155 19s. at the stands (1s. admission) in the League International, played at the Celtic ground on 8th April, 1893.' and:

'Record for Goals scored – The Arbroath in the first round of the Scottish Challenge Cup on the 5th September, 1885, at Arbroath, beat the Bon-Accord of Aberdeen by 36 goals to 0. The next highest was in the same competition, on the same day, at Dundee, when the Harp beat the Aberdeen Rovers by 35 goals to 0.' and:

'Record for playing Scottish Cup ties – George Gillespie (Queen's Park) has played for the Scottish Cup for 18 consecutive years, beginning Rangers v 1st L.R.V. in 1875–6 and ending Queen's Park v Hearts, 1892–3.'

NIGHTMARE AT WEMBLEY

Perhaps it all started too well!

At last, on May 24, 1975, Scotland's fans felt that Wembley was going to be wonderful, that we had at last found a team who could beat England.

And certainly we all believed we had in tall Stewart Kennedy, that brilliant Ranger, a goalkeeper in the mould of Jimmy Cowan and Jerry Dawson, the right man to fill Scotland's problem position.

Manager Willie Ormond's team had gained in confidence with a fine draw against powerful Wales at Cardiff and an impressive victory over Ireland at Hampden. Even without the stars of Leeds United, who were unavailable because their club was playing in the European Cup Final in Paris against Bayern Munich the following Wednesday, Scotland looked solid, strong in defence, skilful in the middle and venomous in attack.

And England, managed by Don Revie, still seemed to be experimenting, lacking balance.

Even the long walk to Wembley – for London's transport workers had gone on strike because of an injury to one of their colleagues the previous Wembley – couldn't damp the spirits of the thousand upon thousand of tartan-tammied fans who made their way to the game.

How were they to know the match would turn into a nightmare? How were they to know the tartan invasion would go into desperate retreat?

But there were no tears at the start. On a bright afternoon, the tartan hordes seethed and swayed up Wembley Way and into the great stadium. Waving their red and yellow banners, knocking back the drams, they left a clattering trail of beer cans and bottles. But they were cheerful and optimistic. And once inside Wembley they turned the arena into a cauldron of noise and tribal emotion. You thought it was an all-Scotland occasion. Hardly an English voice seemed to be raised. Although there were officially only 30 000 Scots at Wembley they seemed to outnumber the home fans by two to one.

It was war again. It was the battle against the ancient enemy they had lived for, prayed for, schemed for, saved up for.

The teams lined up like this:

England – Clemence (Liverpool), Whitworth (Leicester), Beattie (Ipswich), Bell (Manchester City), Watson (Sunderland), Todd (Derby County), Ball(Arsenal) Channon (Southampton), Johnson, (Ipswich), Francis (Queen's Park Rangers), Keegan (Liverpool).

Scotland – Kennedy (Rangers), Jardine (Rangers), McGrain (Celtic), Munro (Wolves), McQueen (Leeds), Rioch (Derby), Dalglish (Celtic), Conn (Spurs), Parlane(Rangers), MacDougall, (Norwich) Duncan (Hibs).

Referee – R. Gloeckner, East Germany.

Although Scotland, captained by Sandy Jardine, who had been chosen not long

Alfie Conn – one of the few players to emerge with credit from Scotland's nightmare. But here Colin Bell trips up the elusive Spurs star as he sets off on yet another run at the English defence.

before as Scotland's Player of the Year, made a fine start, it took only a few minutes for the fans' dreams of glory to end harshly and abruptly and the Scottish carnival, the great carousal, was over.

For Scotland were buried alive and the team died suddenly. And once again, just as it had been for Fred Martin, just as it had been for Frank Haffey, Wembley became the graveyard for yet another fine goalkeeper, Stewart Kennedy.

Although our fans over-ran Wembley with their flags and their chauvinistic exuberance, the England players weren't in the least bit impressed – and Scotland's team weren't in the hunt.

Extraordinary goalkeeping errors by the usually cool Kennedy, who had been the outstanding 'keeper in Britain all season, gave England almost instant domination of the 93rd meeting of the countries and though Scotland remained lively opponents for a long time confidence ebbed away swiftly in the second half and England's winning of the home championship – which we all thought was in Scotland's grasp before the game – was ultimately marked by a scoreline that must, alas, take its place among the more memorable hidings inflicted on the English ground.

It was yet another in a long line of Scottish wakes – all the more disastrous as it had come at a time when the scent of victory over the auld foe was in the air.

But poor Kennedy froze and black memories of the 9—3 slaughter and unfortunate Frank Haffey rose like poisoned clouds in the minds of the Scottish fans as the ball was twice sent beyond the 'keeper, who looked as though he was rooted to a single spot on his goal-line.

How could you believe that Stewart had been a magnificent performer for Scotland against Wales and Northern Ireland in the championship? Had an ankle injury or pain killing injections anything to do with it? Impossible to say anything, except that Wembley does strange things to some players.

Anyhow, only five minutes of the annual ritual had gone when England threw their first spear. From a long and deliberate clearance by Ray Clemence, a goal was born. Mike Channon summoned speed of thought and intelligence to ram a quick pass through to Gerry Francis, who was to become a confident charging bull of a player. He wheeled away to an arc on his right and drove in a shot from 20 yards. It should have been comfortably saved, but astonishingly, the ball was allowed to tuck itself away near the far stanchion.

That, however, was not all of this blue prelude to an unforgettable four-goal first half. Two minutes later, Ball, showing his old touches of experience and leadership, tossed a spectacular pass to Keegan on the right wing.

The Liverpool winger, back in the Revie fold after a walk-out, showed his gratitude for the manager's benevolence by showing Scotland his heels and his centre was met at the far post by the onrushing Beattie. Where was Kennedy?

As the header came to rest in the net the big 'keeper lay prostrate on the grass, utterly dejected by such early misfortune.

It was unbelievable. Scotland had started well enough – and now they were astonishingly two goals down. Gift goals. Goals that came from seemingly nowhere.

Scotland showed her mettle. The great fans, tired though they were from that marathon walk from the city centre, urged them on.

A wonderful sprint through the middle by the magical Ken Dalglish, at last revealing all his skill in the international arena, brought a roar of hope. When his pass gave Derek Parlane a clear run, the cries reached a crescendo. Unfortunately, the Rangers' leader's drive struck the outside of a post as Clemence dived and the ball spun away.

Scotland desperately needed inspiration. There were clever flicks from Dalglish and Alfie Conn, the former Ranger who had been making a name for himself with Spurs, but there was no real fight and England went even further ahead in the 41st minute.

Bell broke through McQueen's tackle and was allowed to steady himself at his leisure and observe that Kennedy was showing two-thirds of his goal on his right side. Bell happily steered the ball through that vast hole.

And England were three up and the game was over.

Just before this goal Scotland might have had a penalty when Bell handled and that would have made a difference. We did, indeed, score from the spot near half-time when Todd put a hand on the ball and Bruce Rioch, who had done so well in previous internationals but who at Wembley sank into becalmed anonimity put the ball past Clemence. By then it was far too late.

Bruce Rioch saves Scotland from a whitewash as he calmly nets the only goal from the penalty spot.

And any slim hope of retrieving an impossible situation vanished early in the second half. Todd again briefly rekindled our optimism with a vague pass back. Arthur Duncan dragged the ball wide into space but his pivoting effort to send it into goal found the wrong side of the net.

Scotland were out of it and the substitution of Hutchison for Duncan did nothing to help.

In fact, it was a foul by Hutchison on Keegan that brought England's fourth goal in the 64th minute. On the edge of the penalty box, England had a chance to show a trick they had been working out in their training headquarters during the week. Ball pushed the ball through Bell's legs and Francis followed up to shoot. Kennedy stood bewildered as the ball was deflected past him.

Our only reply was to replace the labouring Ted MacDougall with Lou Macari.

But spirit had vanished, skill had gone.

Only Conn who launched himself on hopeful runs through the middle looked as though he could do anything.

And England scored again. Danny McGrain, whose earlier excellence was gradually being eroded by the overall decline of his colleagues, fouled Channon deep on Scotland's left. Ball's free kick gave Keegan a free header. Kennedy could only nudge the ball on to the bar. Watson met the rebound, playing the ball against a post and Johnson stepped in to complete a day of misery for the Scotland defence.

England almost scored a sixth when Johnson swept past Munro and gave Channon a wonderful chance. But the attacker failed and the score at the finish was 5—1.

Shades of the Wembley Wizards who had won by that score so many years ago.

Scotland in 1975 were the Wembley Lizards.

It was one of our blackest international days – and even before the kick-off there was trouble for Scotland when Martin Buchan, of Manchester United, decided that as he hadn't been picked as sweeper in preference to Francis Munro of Wolves he wouldn't go to Rumania the following week for the European Championship match in Bucharest.

What annoyed so many Scots was the fact that England were by no means a great side, though obviously better than us. As manager Willie Ormond said ruefully at the end: 'England had six real attempts at goal – and scored from five of them.'

Even in overwhelming defeat, though, the clans never lost their collective voice. They were amazing, those dancing, jigging flamboyantly dressed warriors from north of the Tweed. Although their team's heart had been plucked out, the visiting army invaded the pitch after the game. They blew horns, laughed, yelled, sang. You would have thought they were celebrating a great win over the Sassenach.

Half an hour after a smiling Don Revie had left the pitch with his victor-

ious team, the last of the Scottish fans chanted their way out of the stadium . . . starting the long journey home, watched by the benign London policemen.

As skipper Alan Ball said: 'What fans these Scots are. But for them I thought we could have won easier. The fans lifted the Scottish players and the 5—1 victory wasn't as easy as it sounds. And Scotland at least tried to attack all the time.'

And the Scots took their defeat like sportsmen, admitted Londoners who had feared violence and hooliganism because of the long walk. But there was none of the expected rioting and wrecking as the Scots went home.

Afterwards, of course, there were the inside stories, the plans of Revie, who said his team had decided to play off the front three, with the midfield men going through to support them.

But it was a Wembley all Scots want to forget. Except Stewart Kennedy, who will have nightmares for years about the game.

But he wasn't the only man to accept blame. There were others and, indeed, only Dalglish, Conn and McGrain emerged with credit from the disaster.

In the early stages, though, Scotland pushed the ball around with more accuracy and devil. But England took their chances. Despite their comfortable lead, they did not demonstrate so much control and command of the game.

Tartan dreams were shattered – and it looked as though fate had stepped in with a grim laugh to upset our aspirations, to show those partisan Scots that too much pride almost invariably takes a fall.

For England weren't, frankly, all that much superior – except perhaps in goal.